KNOW WHY

Systems Thinking and Modeling

Gain insights for a happier life, more intelligent management, and a better world

Herstellung und Verlag:
BoD-Books on Demand, Norderstedt
ISBN: 978-3-8482-1430-3

Kai Neumann

KNOW WHY

Systems Thinking and Modeling

Gain insights for a happier life, more intelligent management, and a better world

Note: For Mac and iPad users there is an interactive and extended version of this work called 'KNOW-WHY and the iMODELER' in the Apple iBooks Store. It is enhanced with more illustrations, direct links onto models (running within the book), and a lot of exercises to learn KNOW-WHY-Thinking and the KNOW-WHY-Method.

Kai Neumann
»KNOW WHY: Systems Thinking and Modeling;
Gain insights for a happier life, more intelligent management and a better world«

Content: Kai Neumann
Cover: Kai Neumann
Graphics: Kai Neumann
Proofreading,
English: Gunilla Zedigh

For more information on KNOW-WHY and the author:
www.know-why.org
info@ilsa.de

(ISBN 978-3848214303)

Content

1.   Our biggest challenge: growing complexity

Our business success, personal happiness and humankind after all depend on our ability to understand the interconnections present within the increasingly complex challenges we face. The economy is on the brink of collapse, there is fierce competition on the job market, more and more people in industrialized nations consider themselves to be unhappier than people in developing countries, and according to studies, earning an annual income of $70,000 or more doesn't make us any happier. We feel the impact of climate change and suffer from the effects of i.e. pollution, war, poverty and depleting resources – despite the fact that we know which measures we need to take to combat them. We need to understand why we do not change.

In order to be successful, we need to know how things are interconnected and also why they are the way they are. This is crucial because very often we know what should have an impact but we do not know why. We therefore need to apply KNOW WHY Thinking.

When something is complex it means that it is largely unpredictable and that it can only be "approximated." We can handle complexity in five different ways: ignore it, lessen it, refer to best practices, use our gut feeling, or do our best to examine it through systemic analysis. Systemic (systems thinking, systems theory and systems modeling) means that we observe a part of reality and try to describe it through an interplay of factors that we include in a mental or computer model. It is well known, however, that we are not able to grasp the interplay of more than four factors without the aid of a tool. This is where modeling with the help of a computer comes in.

Modeling can be grouped into two categories: quantitative (system dynamics, agent based modeling, neural networks) and qualitative modeling. Both allow us to analyze the impact of causal chains and feedback loops, which are either reinforcing or balancing and cause dynamic developments.

While quantitative modeling works with data and formulas and results in scenario simulations that predict a system's behavior over time, the less sophisticated qualitative modeling only roughly describes the connections between factors. It yields matrices that allow us to compare the influences that factors have. Qualitative modeling with a new tool like the iMODELER promises to be the first tool easy enough to be routinely used by planners and decision makers, in fact by all of us from schoolchildren to families to presidents.

The insights we gain from cause and effect modeling depend on how we observe "reality," the factors that we include and the connections that we see. We need to apply our knowledge, the knowledge from others (e.g. from KNOW-WHY.NET), creativity, our gut feeling even and a method that helps us to find the crucial factors. This is why we should use the KNOW WHY Method, which is based on KNOW WHY Thinking.

Unfortunately, many systems thinkers do not gain insights because they use a tool. Instead, they use a tool to merely demonstrate their view in descriptive models and then go on to claim that their interpretation has authority the same way that many reductionist thinkers do. However, a new tool like the iMODELER – that even runs on your smartphone – together with the KNOW WHY Method and KNOW-WHY.NET allows us all to gain new insights from explorative models on a daily basis.

What we usually do when faced with challenges: reduce the number of factors.

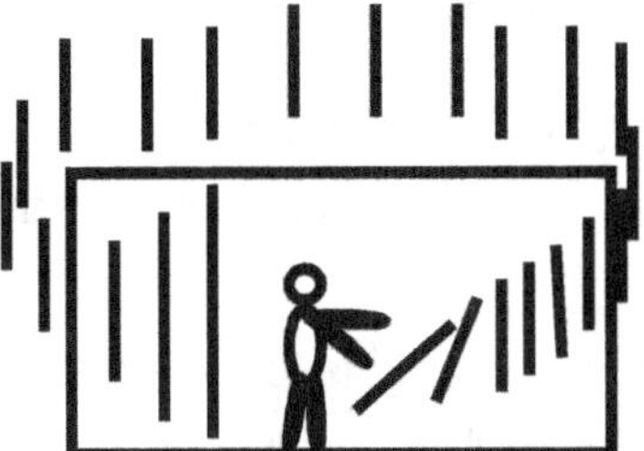

In reality, however, the interconnections of many factors allow small influences to have a large impact.

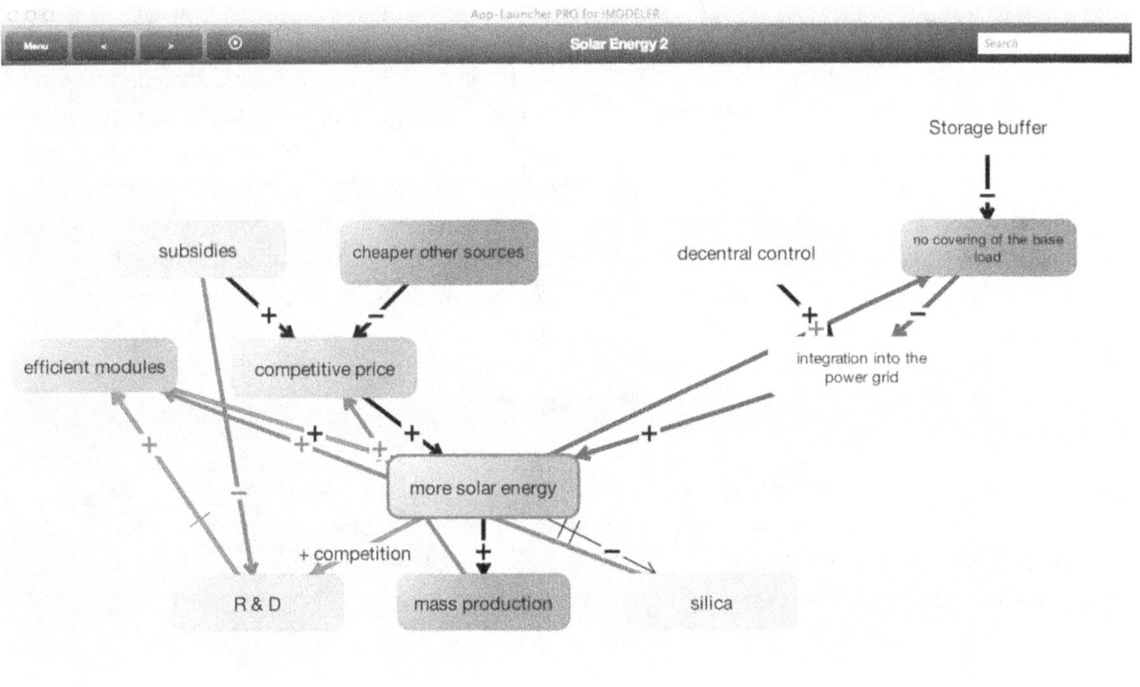

A small cause and effect model showing reenforcing (more solar energy, more R&D, more efficient modules, more solar energy) and balancing (more solar energy, more no covering of the base load, less integration into the power grid, less (!) more solar energy) feedback loops

2.   Giving up: gut feeling and best practices

It is only natural and thus (!) logical that we dislike the uncertainty that accompanies complexity. We also dislike most arduous work – and not just because we lack the time for it. We basically like to keep things simple and to keep the number of factors in our mental or computer model to a minimum, too. We also tend to refer to best practices, or listen to our gut feeling.

But reducing the number of factors is a mistake. Keep it short and simple (KISS) works for communication but not for analysis. The law of variety (W.R. Ashby) states that we need to level the number of possible states that we can take with that of reality. Inconspicuous factors might trigger crucial feedback loops, however, and hence we shouldn't shy away from building or thinking in terms of very large models. Creativity also increases through the visualization of many factors. We can "bisociate," meaning that we can form new ideas by combining different associations. Of course, we need a tool that allows us to handle the many factors.

Best practice solutions are based on valuable knowledge. But knowledge that was valid in the past under different circumstances may not necessarily be applicable to a given situation in the present or future. If it were, success could simply be attained by copying from the best.

Our gut feeling, or intuitive intelligence, is a mighty mechanism from nature. We are able to use our experiences from the past to unconsciously reach conclusions in the present. We abstract from what we have learned and develop a feeling for a situation that is similar. It is almost a reflex and therefore very difficult to reconstruct how we got our gut feeling – a feeling that depends on three things: our experiences, our perception of the circumstances surrounding the challenge we face and – as it is a feeling – the emotional state we are in. This is also the reason that our gut feeling might at times be less based on past experiences and biased by our present feelings. If we are in a bad mood we judge things differently than when we are in a good mood. Our unconscious perception of certain aspects is limited to the present. And we cannot predict future outcomes because they depend on aspects from the future. Unfortunately, many publications on gut feelings lack this insight. Last but not least, the benefit provided by a gut feeling in dealing with a complex challenge depends not just on the number of past experiences we have had but also on our experiences with nonlinear developments that arise from feedback loops. We can see such cause and effects when we model.

Cause and effect models often do not include only factual knowledge and hence we need to use our gut feeling to judge the weight of one factor's effect on another factor. If we have no gut feeling, we simply have to guess. But this is perfectly okay, too, because we aren't guessing the behavior of an entire system. We can truly only benefit from modeling.

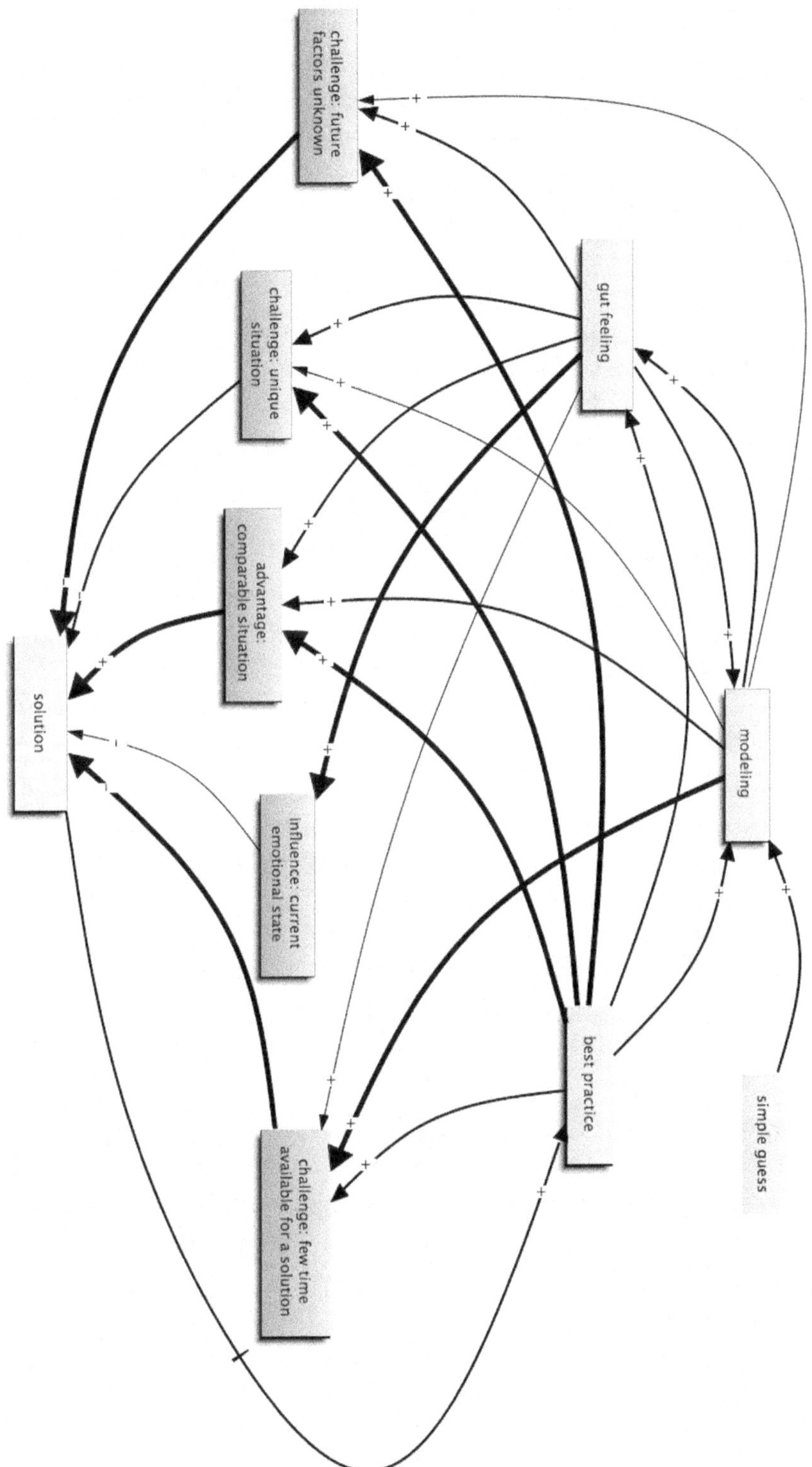

A combination of best practices, gut feeling and modeling works best as they are interdependent of each other.

3.   Why things are: The KNOW-WHY-Thinking

There are numerous systems theories out there. Most of them, however, e.g. the viable systems model (Stafford Beer), AGIL (Talcott Parsons) and the ideas of Niklas Luhmann merely describe how some systems work. They don't describe WHY things work the way they do and so these theories cannot explain why any given system will be successful or fail. Another drawback: many theories are much too complicated to be used in actual planning and decision-making situations.

To understand why something is successful or not, and to provide a simple mind tool for this kind of reflection, I have developed KNOW WHY Thinking. It is based on the evolutionary logic that everything in the world must both adapt to its environment (integration) and change (development) when its environment changes, or for the sake of competition. If, at least in the long run, something lacks either integration or development its existence will be jeopardized. There is no survival of the fittest involved here – survival is guaranteed by simply "fitting in" because there is both integration and development. This evolutionary pattern of success applies to simply everything: products, strategies, organizations, individuals, societies, relationships, etc. Integration and Development – there has to be both to prevent catastrophe.

I have created the KNOW WHY Wave to make thinking in these terms easier. This wave is an iconographic representation of the success of something. The top of the wave depicts maximum success. To reach the top of the wave there needs to be development. Too much development without integration, however, is catastrophic and will cause something to fall right off of the wave. Without any development the wave might move on, resulting in a decrease in success.

You can use the KNOW WHY Wave for just about everything. Grab a newspaper and for every topic you read about ask yourself whether the "problem" being addressed is due to too much development (meaning a lack of integration), or by a lack of development (meaning that there has been no movement beyond the environment where integration initially took place). Sounds trivial? Give it a try. Foreign military interventions without the integration of the local people. Tablet computers with new operating systems but no apps. Schools that deny climate change and evolution. Shifting towards renewable energies without a smart grid. A financial market decoupled from the real economy. The exponential growth of content in social networks. The growth of the Chinese economy. And so forth and so on …

Where on a wave would you, for example, place the Catholic Church, e-mobility, peace in Israel, the fishing industry, the UN, the EU, yourself? It is perfectly okay if you are ambiguous about some of your answers. You can model them using the KNOW WHY Method (please see chapter 5) and then you can discuss your results with others to develop a common mental model.

It is much easier, of course, to reflect on something after the fact than to foresee the success of something in advance. KNOW WHY Thinking will, however, definitely lead to more success than any gut feeling ever will. We just need to get used to think of something and its position on the wave before it is happening.

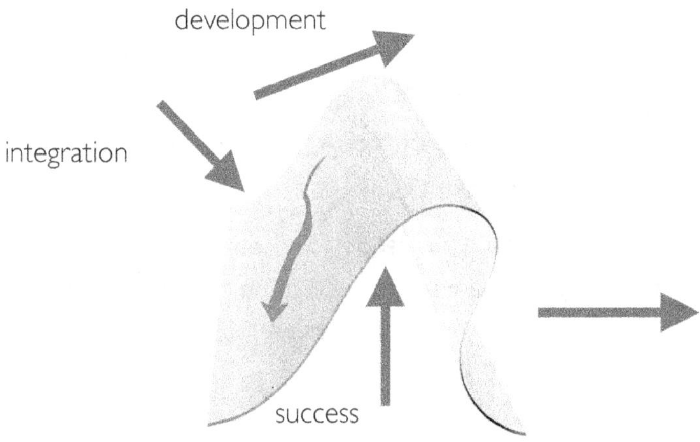

Without development the wave will move on and we will be less successful

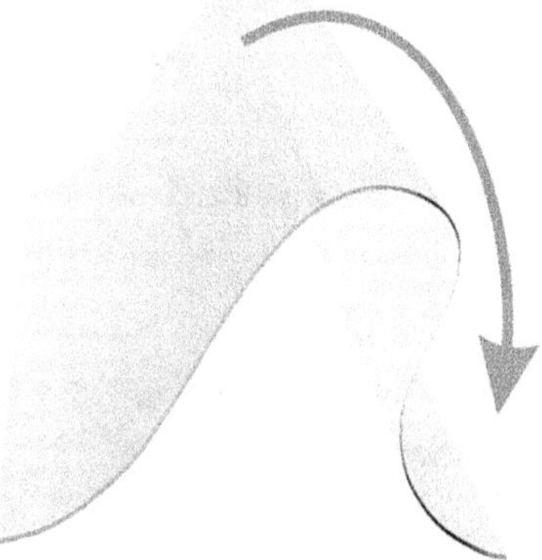

Too much development without integration will cause us to fall off of the wave and not be successful at all.

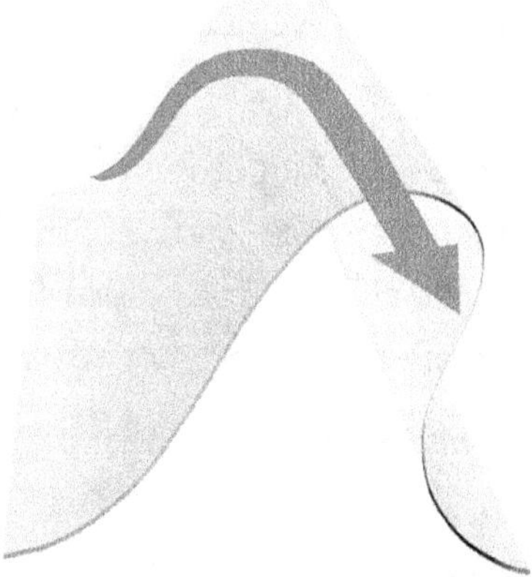

Integrated development leads to a maximum success at the top of the wave

4.   The KNOW WHY of human motivation

Just like all things, we individuals (and also humankind as a whole) need to integrate and develop to be successful. Generally speaking, we are able to do this because we are either following orders, act after having given a situation a great deal of thought, or because a good feeling guides us. (https://www.know-why.net/model/Atxrf7zQLpoe5JP2Uvumyjw)

In chapter 9, I go into more detail on how free will and consciousness works. Emotional motivation figures in the most: evolution gave us emotions through hormones and neurotransmitters. There are things we like and dislike, and things we fear. Interestingly enough, any feeling can be regarded as a sign of our feelings of integration or development. Feelings also tell us if our integration or happiness is being jeopardized. There is no feeling that cannot be linked to the evolutionary logic of KNOW WHY. Of course, humans need to integrate with other humans. Our will to develop drives civilization – yielding both good and bad accomplishments.

The conditions that make us feel integrated or that we are developing are totally arbitrary. For some people playing video games or chatting online affects the same neurotransmitters as building a house or playing soccer with friends does for others. Our friends, conversations, careers, gadget purchases, book reading habits, desire to own a pet, fandom and subcultures with rituals are all very important, as are religion and fashion trends, etc. because we have an evolutionary need to feel integrated and that we are developing. Depression, boredom, anxiety, hyperactivity, drug use, etc. are all due to a lack of integration or development. Feeling integrated or that we are developing by identifying with fictitious TV and video game characters, for instance, means living passively and vicariously. It is a vicious circle, because our real lives will never be as great, but just as with those intense feeling we experience when taking drugs, here too we escape from the burdens of real life and drift into passivity.

Other concepts that explain human motivation (Maslow's pyramid, Spiral Dynamics, McClelland's basic motives, Schwartz's universal values etc.) describe in some cases even bio-psychologically the behavior of some humans. They don't explain the KNOW WHY of everyone's behavior..

Interestingly enough, there is often a conflict between the things we want to do and the things we have to do, the latter of which requires energy and discipline. Being happy because we feel integrated and that we are developing in life gives us energy. Discipline on the other hand is very much like a muscle – it must be trained, and after a long, exhausting day it often loses strength.

You can even compare cultures with each other. In many Asian cultures, for example, integration is emphasized, while in others (most Western societies) development prevails. The prior would benefit from a greater degree of freedom and the latter from increased integration through values.

Social as well as individual pathologies can be understood (please see chapter 11), when we reflect on the integration and development of people as individuals. In the following chapters, you will see how human motivation is pivotal to understanding wars, environmental pollution and much more.

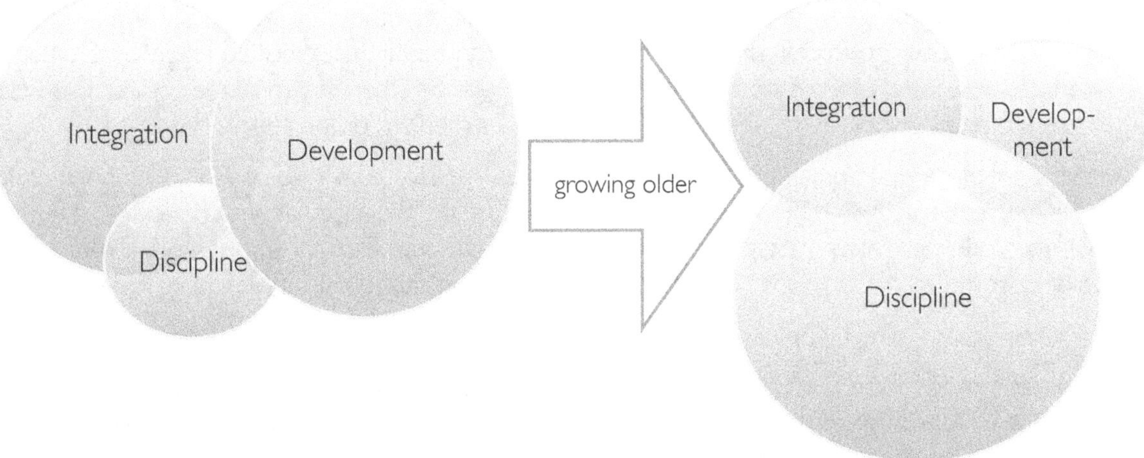

For many people as they grow older discipline prevails over feelings.

Do you have everything you need? Think of what integrates you, what develops you, what bores you and what frightens you.

5. Qualitative modeling: beyond mind mapping

We need cause and effect modeling because of our mental limits. While quantitative modeling is comparably sophisticated, qualitative modeling (using the revolutionary iMODELER) is as easy as mind mapping (though mind mapping merely shows content without analyzing it). We link so-called factors with arrows to form an argument. The arrows can be further specified to describe whether one factor causes another factor to increase or decrease, whether the impact is comparable weak, medium or strong short term, and whether this changes medium or long term.

Anything can be a factor and we should use natural language, apply no special rules nor opt for specific types of factors to model what we are thinking and/or speaking about. This lowers the entry level to modeling, makes it easy to talk about the models and leads to surprisingly valid models – which become valid if all connections can be described with the following sentence:

"More of factor x directly (!) leads to more/less of factor y."

Qualitative models are in most cases undisputed because everyone can easily agree on the fuzzy weighting whether something is a comparably weak or strong influence on a factor. There is no discussion as to the exact value of a parameter within a formula for a quantitative model.

If the individual arguments are correct and complete, the analysis of the logical sum should be correct, too. To include the crucial factors with your model you should apply the KNOW WHY Method and to get proposals for possible influences on each factor use KNOW-WHY.NET.

We analyze a model using the iMODELER'S unique Insight Matrix. In this Insight Matrix we can see how a given factor in the model is influenced by the other factors. An influencing factor's position on the horizontal axis is the sum of the impact of all its connections that lead to the given factor. The position on the vertical axis is the change of the impact of the influencing factor caused by feedback loops and delays. If reinforcing feedback loops (e.g., more money leads to higher interest rates, which leads to more money …) prevail, the impact increases – sometimes even exponentially. If balancing feedback loops (e.g., more money leads to a higher living standard, which leads to less money …) prevail, the impact decreases, and eventually it even results in the opposite effect.

The values for weak, very weak, medium, strong and very strong depend on the number of influencing factors. If for example there are 5 influencing factors the medium impact is 20. The position of a factor in the Insight Matrix, then, simply shows whether a factor has more or less of an impact than other factors do. Whether it is absolutely positive or negative can only be ascertained if we use absolute percentage values for the weightings instead of rough relative values. That, of course, might take more time effort.

A model simply shows what would be the case if all of the arguments are correct. and complete It shows the likely outcome – but do not forget that the nature of complexity makes it impossible to predict an outcome one hundred percent. However, any model is better than no model.

Go to www.iMODELER.net, www.imodeler.info or www.know-why.net to give it a try.

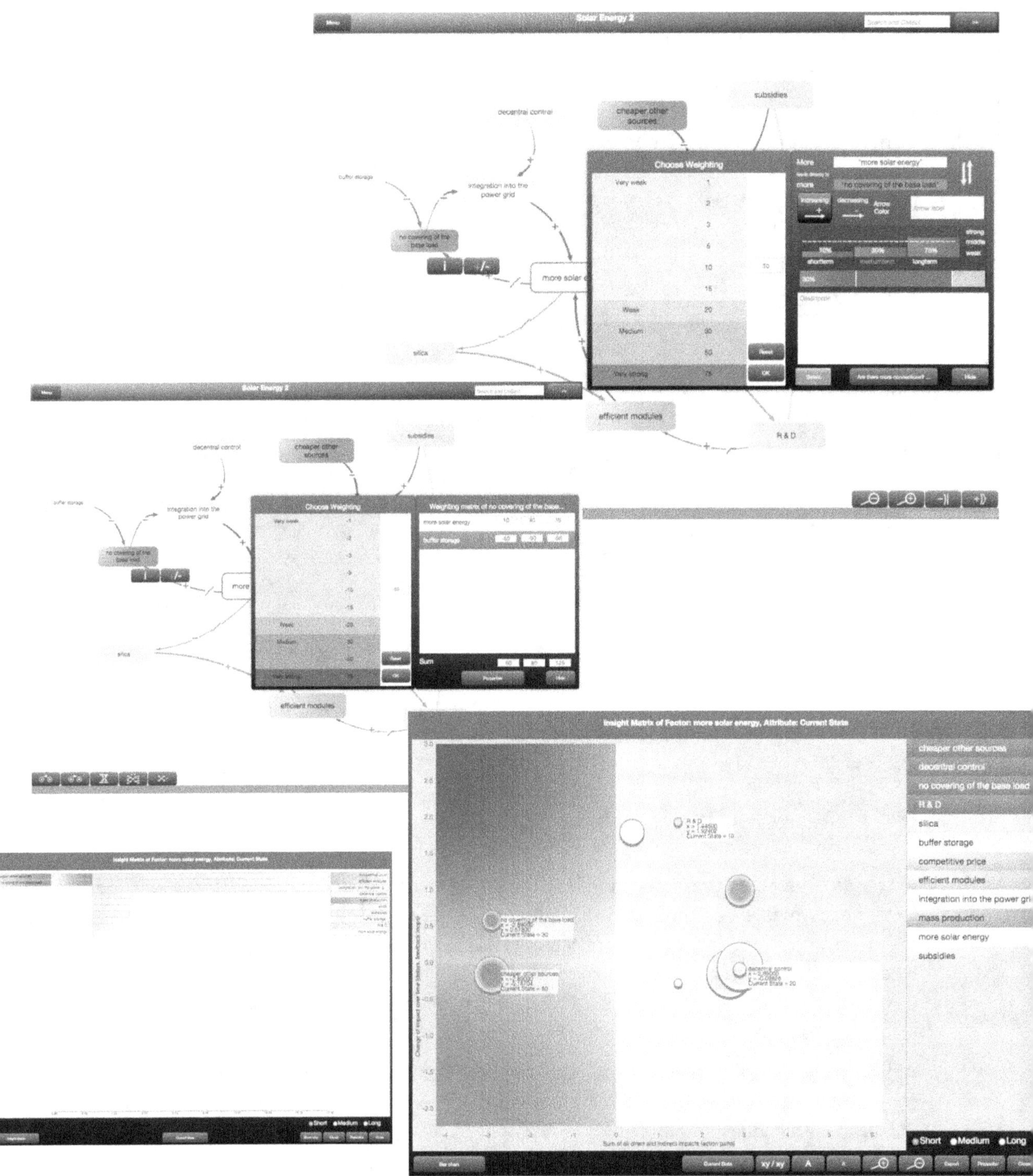

Qualitative modeling, rough weighting, the Insight Matrix and Bar Charts showing the matrix' values.

6.   The KNOW-WHY-method: systemic and systematic modeling

A model is valid if the following sentence applies to every connection in it: "More of ... directly leads to more/less of ..." A good model also needs to contain crucial factors. As mentioned earlier, many modelers begin by simply modeling what they think they know. But in order to be able to discover some important — and maybe even new — insights, a model needs to include crucial factors, which we can only discover through background knowledge and by applying our creativity. Using the KNOW WHY Method we can systematically ask ourselves which factors we know are involved and then brainstorm to come up with factors that might be crucial as well. This process is also systemic as it serves to explicitly or implicitly ask for the factors that define the integration or the development of a factor. Interestingly enough, no important factor will not either have an impact on the integration or the development of another factor.

Here is how it works: start off with a target factor that describes that which you are trying to find out how it can be achieved. Then ask yourself the following questions:

●   What directly leads to more of it?

After you have connected the answers (as factors) using arrows and validated the connection by making sure that the sentence "more of ... directly leads to more/less of ..." applies, ask yourself:

●   What directly leads to less of it? What hinders or makes this factor decrease?

... followed by:

●   What leads to more /is needed for more of this factor in the future?

... and finally:

●   What might happen in the future that could cause this factor to decrease/lead to less of it?

Once we have asked these questions for the target factor we continue by also asking them for each factor that we have come up with. I advise that this be done level by level and not in depth because the most important factors are probably in close proximity to the target factor. You must decide when you think that you have attained enough details so that you can ignore any further impacts. Of course, you should continue to model until your factors include concrete actions that can be taken to gain success.

Although the question technique should already lead to such actions you may be required to explicitly ask yourself how you can achieve integration or development for a given factor in order to come up with effective measures for your target.

Also you should consider to click on the KNOW-WHY.NET button when defining a new incoming connection in order to get some proposals from the worldwide community of modelers.

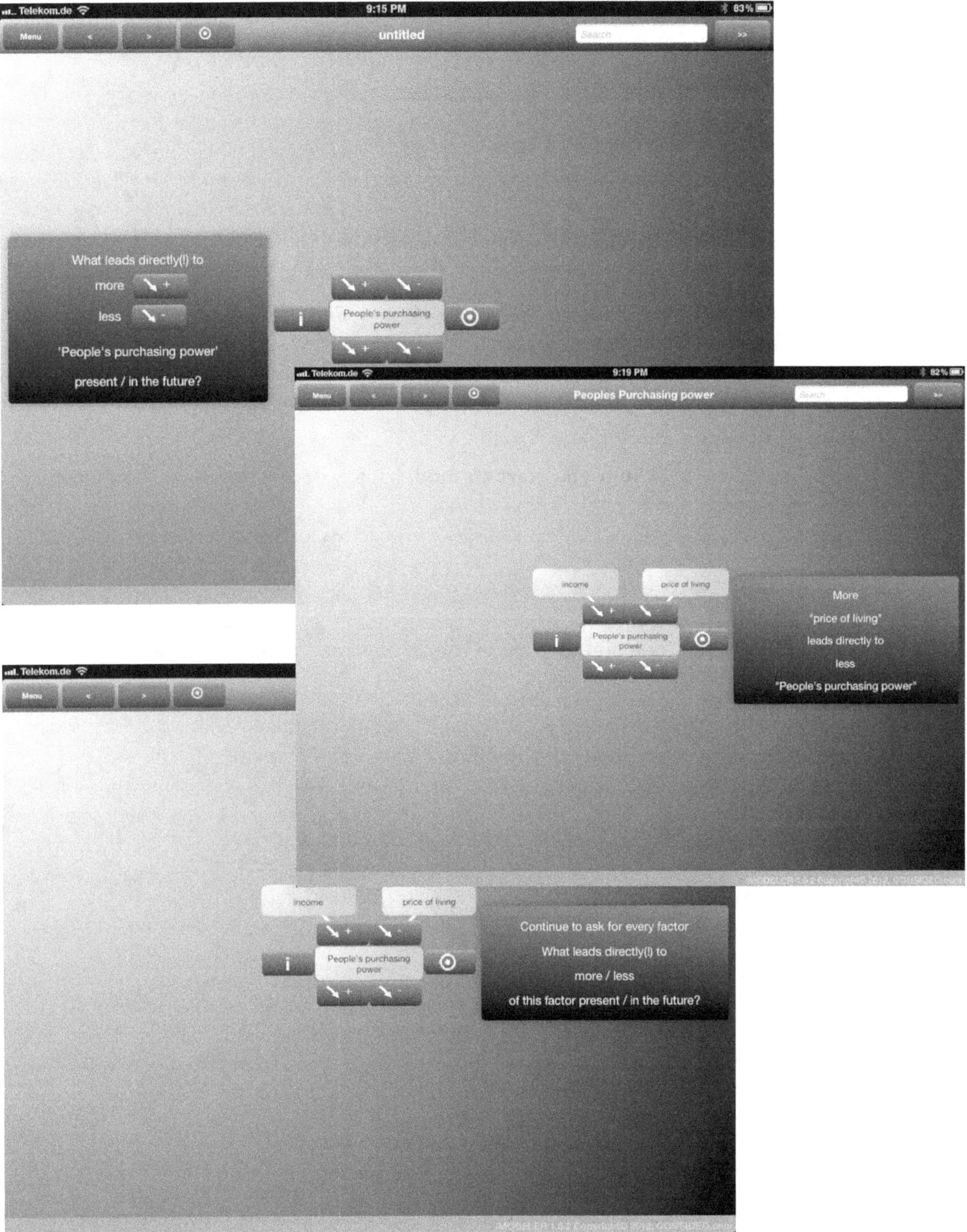

The start of a model guided by the iMODELER. Following it leads automatically to a valid model!

7. Tips and tricks on modeling

If you have a completely new task, begin by thinking of a structure for the model. This will limit the model's size and development. For example, say you have a goal that is divided into subgoals and is influenced by processes that also influence each other. The processes are dependent on resources, and both the resources and the processes might be influenced by incidents. One major goal of the model might be to look for activities that can handle these incidents. Enter this structure into a **mini-model in the iMODELER** or on a whiteboard. You can use the mini- model as the basis for your color coding and categories as well.

If you **want to compare alternative solutions** simply use a model structure that puts the solutions at the beginning of the cause chains ending in the overall benefit, thus telling you how each of the solutions influences different criteria, triggers certain dynamics, and, of course, how they influence the costs. The position in the Insight Matrix, then, shows the best solution.

Think carefully with **whom you start to model**. If the challenge you want to model, for example, is new to everyone in a team it is advisable to tap the full creative potential of this large, interdisciplinary group. If the most important factors for a given topic are well known, however, you can start to model together with only the experts on the topic at hand so that the others don't get bored. If you fear that modeling with certain members of a group might lead to unproductive discussions on details, you can opt to model with the generalists only. However, your first draft of a model should be shared with a large number of people and be refined by their input.

If you have **prepared lists** of possible factors from other methodologies, e.g. brainstorming, metaplan technique, etc., **don't use them** right away! Yes, you can expect that everyone will moan that you are doubling the workload, but it is very likely that you will otherwise need to rename the factors if you decide to put them into a cause and effect relationship. It is also the case that concentrating on how to connect existing factors will keep you from thinking freely about the factors that are actually important. This does not mean, however that everything you prepared in a previous work session, for example, was for naught. You can crosscheck the factors you have added to your model with the list of factors you compiled earlier.

Always make sure to **ask only what influences a factor** and not what a factor influences. It is almost inevitable that a group of modelers will get lost if one of them switches back and forth and models in both directions. Many less experienced users try modeling without following this advice and fail. Even experienced users who ignore this advice will often find themselves surprised by the results that are obtained.

If you have the feeling that the name of a factor is too arbitrary, then you should ask yourself **how it might possibly be measured**. This helps to give it just the right name.

- Whenever you discuss a factor or a connection, make sure to **add a description text** to it so that you and others can later easily understand why you modeled the way you did.

- As I mentioned earlier, it is best to start modeling with your main target factor **level by level**. Factors that are far away from the main factor may only have a minor impact, and quite often models tend to become much too detailed for one aspect. Modelers risk running out of time – time that is needed to model other aspects.

- Begin by **connecting** the factors, then **color code** (e.g. through categories) them and then **weight** their connections. Color coding means making factors that you want to compare with each other in the Insight Matrix the same color.

- Optional: **use quantitative attributes to add another dimension** to your model – via its properties every factor can get quantitative attributes to express, e.g., the status of a task in a project or the likelihood that an incident might happen. This enables you, for instance, to see in the Insight Matrix that a risk is very high on account of its impact, but very unlikely because of its color. You will also be able to see that an already completed task in a project is very important, but that an uncompleted one is not that important.

- If you add some details in a description text for the connections and/or factors as an alternative to additional factors you may find yourself with a **smaller model** and thus be able to model more quickly.

- If you face time limitations and therefore get frustrated by the level of detail that work session participants are adding to a model, try asking them to give you **general terms** that describe a group of other detailed factors. For example, if there are eight ways that industry pollutes the environment, and you see no need to look at the detailed factors such as air, water, soil, radiation, etc., then after participants state the first factor ask them if it might be possible to include this factor together with a number of others factors and then call this one factor "pollution of environment." Generalize first – and once the model has quickly been completed, you can still go back and add in details. This method is much better than running the risk of having to terminate a project with unfinished models that have a high level of detail.

- In many cases you or the people you are modeling with will opt to start at the first level with a large number of **allegedly directly influencing factors**. Even if you as a facilitator don't agree that they are directly influencing the target of the model, if the others insist on this connection then let them. Later, when you ask them what directly leads to the existing factors, they will again mention factors that are already directly connected and you will have more than one connection between the factor and the target. If a connection basically means the same thing then the direct (!) connection is redundant.

- A model, especially a qualitative one that **uses natural language**, is like a written text. There are days when you feel that your first draft is perfect, but other days when you find yourself reworking it over and over again. As with any text you must distance yourself from the model for at least two days or have someone else take a look at your model and give you feedback. You know your thoughts and ideas; it is your mental model. However, whether it can be understood by others – including you after some time has passed – is not always a sure thing. When you ask with a new influence on a factor <u>KNOW-WHY.NET</u> via the magic button that may work as an advice from others.

- As the saying goes: garbage in, garbage out. If you are not in top form, the model might yield nonsense. However, if the sentence "more of … directly leads to more/less of …" is correct for every connection within you model, then the model is correct. Whether the model is useful depends on your inclusion of the crucial factors. That's what the KNOW WHY Method and its four questions and also <u>KNOW-WHY.NET</u> are for.

- If your expert knowledge or **your gut feeling disagrees** with the results you get from the Insight Matrix then take a closer look at your model. Small oversights might lead to completely different results, e.g., a mistake in the polarity of a connection. If the model is valid you have learned something new and your gut feeling or knowledge will have been proven wrong.

- A model can easily become very large as it might display all the thoughts you and your team have on a topic and the world around you. If you later present this large model to others it would literally mean "too much development without integration" for them. As far as presenting your results to others is concerned, you should make sure to only **show parts of your model** in detail. If possible, ask an audience for their opinion on some of your connections or ask them what they would think the crucial factors at a selected point of your model are and then show them the factors you have included. Asking is a way of leading. The complete model is merely an illustration of how much work you have done. Especially in the case of the Insight Matrix, you should select only a few factors you want to compare. As with any project presentation, of course, you should create a story that integrates your audience or reader: What was your goal? What is the result? What did you do? Why is it so? Again, what is the result? What should be done next? And by whom?

- In the history of modeling there are numerous examples of experts having built sophisticated models yielding astonishing results yet actual decision-makers then making decisions that were completely independent of these results. Their decisions were based on a gut feeling or on best practices from the past. Actually sitting down and analyzing a challenge at hand was something they didn't do. The implication of this is that a result was only accepted if it matched their gut feeling – otherwise it was rejected, because it meant "too much development without integration." This goes to show that you should try to **integrate the actual decision-maker**. Let them join in on the modeling session. Ask them if they agree with the relationships and weightings of a few select details. Ask them, don't tell them. The iMODELER with its use of natural language is easy enough to be used and understood by everyone. Almost every decision maker has a smartphone or a tablet. With the iMODELER they can make use of it :-)

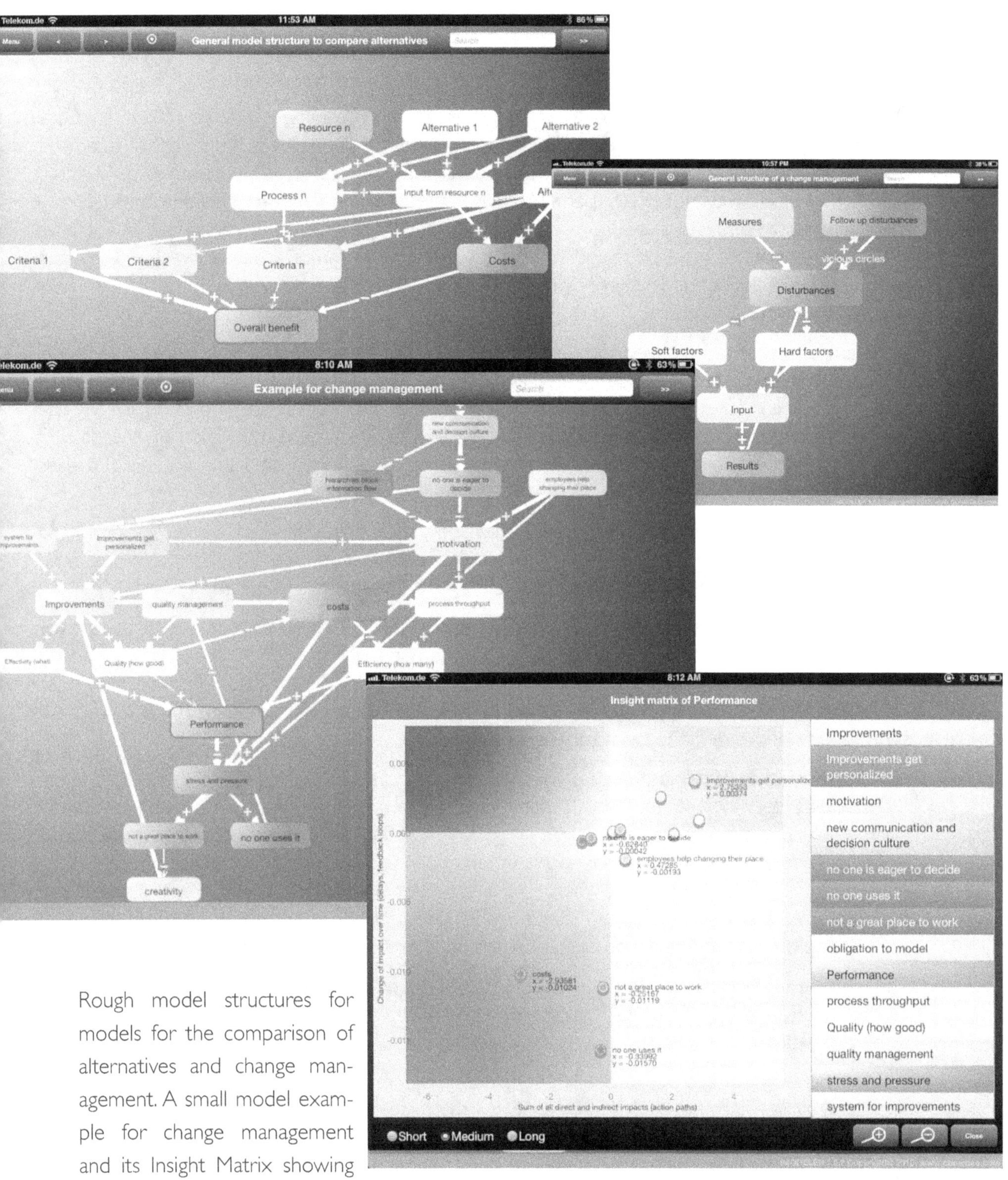

Rough model structures for models for the comparison of alternatives and change management. A small model example for change management and its Insight Matrix showing how important factors are while their color gradients show the current state of them.

8.   Quantitative modeling

The challenge of identifying the crucial factors for quantitative modeling is the same as it is for qualitative modeling. Disagreeing with some classical approaches, I recommend that you take the natural language approach for quantitative modeling, too. Quantitative modeling is more sophisticated. We need to gather data, develop mathematical formulas and know or agree on concrete parameters, but it rewards us with potentially better results. While qualitative models and the Insight Matrix merely suggest what factors are more or less important for the target in your model, quantitative models can suggest at what point and with what value a target can be reached. In cases where the parameters of many factors are unknown and you know that your time is limited, it might be better to opt for qualitative modeling.

If there are soft factors involved such as motivation, popularity, etc., then it is very useful to model them without a unit with values between 0 and 1. To connect factors that have no units with factors that do, e.g., the motivation of employees with the number of mistakes in a production line, we can use a so-called relation editor to graphically sketch how, for instance, a motivation of 1 leads to 3 mistakes per day while a motivation of 0.5 leads to 80 mistakes per day and a motivation of 0 leads to 300 mistakes per day.

If you have many soft factors or you want to develop your model very quickly, you can opt for the "relative quantification" of a qualitative model, which means that you transfer all possible qualitative weightings from the connections into the formula, e.g., 0.25*factor x + 0.1*factor y.

For more realistic results – and greater acceptance from people who are skeptical that complexity can be simulated – use a so-called Monte Carlo simulation that will give you not just one scenario but a bandwidth of possible outcomes. This means that you won't need to define a fixed value for a single parameter but instead determine that variation is possible. The iMODELER will calculate a series of simulations randomly with varying parameters.

Although you can use a wide range of formulas, in most cases all you need are a few basic arithmetic operations. However, it is worth mentioning the range() function. You can use it to find an optimal solution to the challenge you face if you have asked what combination of values leads to it. Simply provide the possible range for each parameter and then allow the tool to try out every possible combination so you can see which one is the most optimal. This method is also called soft operations research. It, too, is quite easy to use for certain kinds of regression analyses when you want to find out what combination of parameters best matches a given set of data from the past.

There are several smart ways to import data into your model – from Excel and by use of the classic MODELER also SQL and OLAP databases, etc. If possible you should validate your model with some real data.

Beyond the scope of this book are the iMODELER's features as a authoring tool for easy to build simulation games, and the PROCESS-iMODELER that features addition types of factors to model projects and processes in order to identify optimal parameters, constraints (ToC) and possible developments of complex processes or projects.

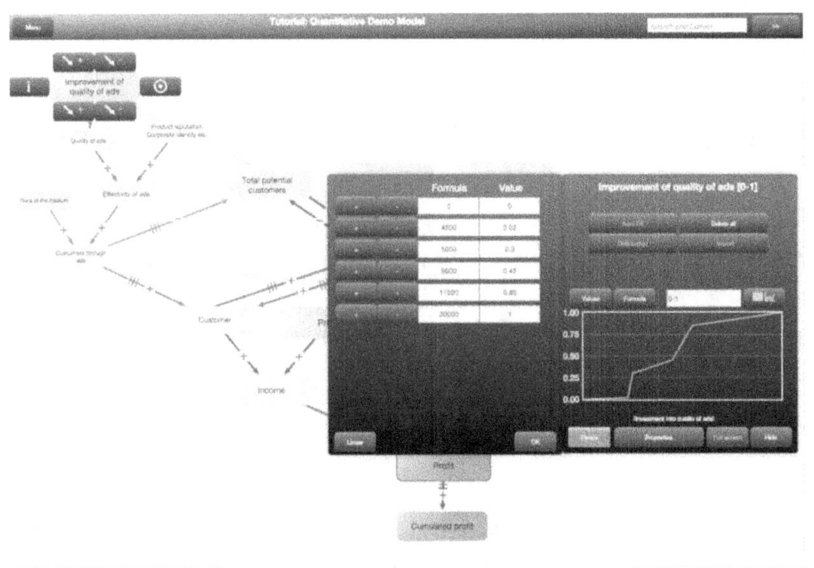

Quantitative model showing the relation editor that allows you to put different units into relation with each other

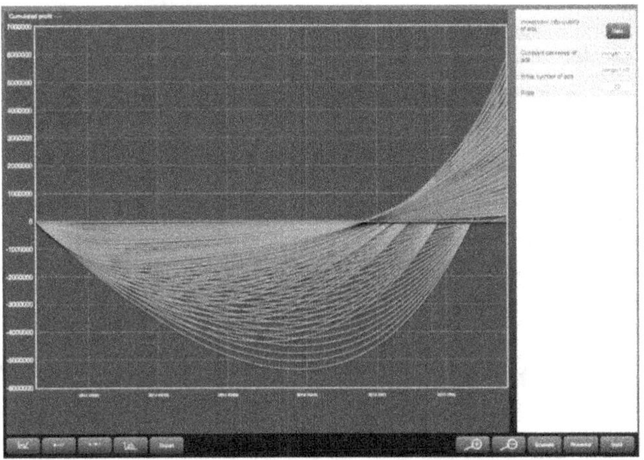

A Monte Carlo simulation showing a range of possible outcomes. You can choose any scenario to see what combination of parameters led to it. You explore best, worst and most likely cases.

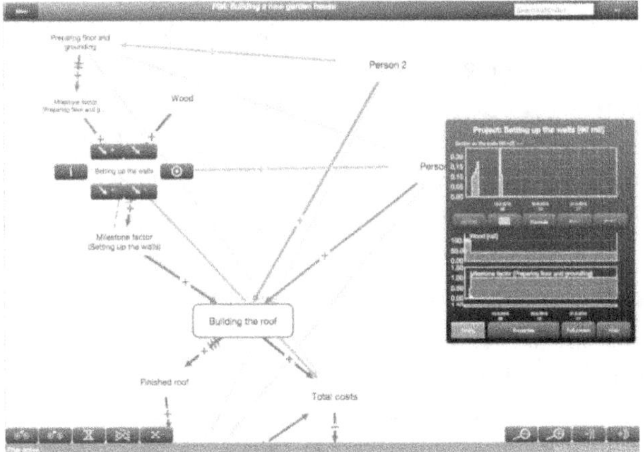

With the PROCESS-iMODELER features of the iMODELER you can easily model complex processes and projects in order to identify optimal parameters (Operations Research) or identify constraints (Theory of Constraints)

9.   Free will, EQ and consciousness

If we are looking for ways to improve our own or other people's happiness we can reflect on it using KNOW WHY. I will explain how in the following chapters. Three aspects need to be considered first upon which our happiness depend: our free will, our emotional intelligence and our ability to act consciously.

Whether we act out of free will or not is an ongoing discussion in philosophy and even in law studies. Applying the KNOW WHY perspective I would venture to say that the romantic idea of free choice does not exist for higher creatures, who are by no means free or autonomous when it comes to feelings of integration and development – feeling, which, in turn, are dependent on the social context the individuals are living in. What we want arises from the context we live in. In principle we can freely choose one thing over something else, but our choice is determined by whether it gives us a feeling of integration or development. This is why most of us share the same values and strive to achieve very similar things in life.

Emotional intelligence means that we have the ability to become aware of our feelings – we know if we feel good or not. Many people are driven by reason ('ratio') and actually have no clue as to their true emotional state. It is quite a sad thing if towards the end of a person's life they realize that they did not actually do what they had wanted to do. Our 'ratio' can indeed block the flow of hormones and neurotransmitters. Many people need alcohol in order to relax and to feel emotions again. The opposite is also quite possible: people need emotional intelligence in order to get a handle on their emotions, which can block 'ratio'. We are all familiar with the feelings of anxiety, anger, ecstasy, etc., for example. Emotional intelligence also means that we have empathy for others and can recognize whether they are being driven by their emotions or if they are fully accountable for their actions. In order to devise a plan for more happiness we thus need to know what feels good and we need to be able to return to 'ratio' if bad feelings keep us from sticking to our plan.

Allegedly, consciousness is unique to human beings. Generally speaking, we are able to reflect on everything we do. We can think of the physical situation, the weight, position, force, material, etc. We can think of what an action means in a social, historical and philosophical context. We can think about how we feel about it. We can think about the existentialist meaning it has for us. Where are we? What are we holding in our hands? What material is this thing made of? How heavy is it? How does it feel in our hands? How do we feel? How quickly are we breathing? However, these questions are endless. It is impossible to reflect on everything that you can possibly reflect on, and that is the main reason why we reflect on only a few things (if on any at all) throughout the course of our lives. Other reasons why many of us do not reflect on a regular basis is that it takes effort, emotional intelligence and it requires that we have background knowledge as well as the ability to think in terms of cause and effect structures. You can do nearly everything without having to reflect on it, and it is actually true that you can do many things better if you don't reflect on them. Just think of a child learning to ride a bicycle. If the child gives riding a bicycle too much thought, he or she will crash. The problem is, however, that we grow accustomed to not reflecting on things and this means that we miss out on many opportunities that could make us more successful and happier in our lives – both of which can be attained through increased consciousness. In principal, of course, we are not required to reflect on anything. And if we do, we only have time to reflect on some of the things that we experience, know and feel. We can probably never be 100 percent conscious.

Exercise 1

Let us try a little exercise: stop reading, close this book for a moment and reflect on it. Be conscious of the fact that you have been reading this book. After you are done return to reading and see what else you might have thought of.

Exercise 2

Here are a few examples of what you can reflect on while reading this book. What is your goal? What do you hope to benefit? What does it mean to your life? What would ensure that you benefit from reading this book? What kind of paper is it made out of? Was the price of the book reasonable? How heavy is the book? Do you like the title and the cover? Where are you sitting right now? How are you holding the book? How do you feel? Who is the author (actually, this is not all that interesting …)? What might the book mean to the world? What could you have done if you hadn't been reading the book?

Likely conclusion

In this example, all that was reflected on was the reading of a book. You can generally reflect on everything you do. However, it is not possible to reflect on something 100%, nor is there any right or wrong way to do it. Nevertheless, we can increase our understanding by reflecting more, and if we do, the probability that we will become more successful and happier increases. We will return to this in chapter 20.

10. Personal happiness: our HIDP

The most important, easiest and most interesting model is arguably your personal holistic integration and development plan (HIDP). All you need to do is have your overall happiness be a central factor and then you connect the factors "felt integration" and "felt development" to it. Once you have done that become conscious and aware of the emotions you are feeling and begin to reflect on what you have in your life (or will have in the near future) that make you feel integrated, and also what threatens your integration. Do the same for your feelings regarding development.

Some typical examples of important factors in your life are your partner, your family, your job, your hobbies, your home and your pets. Trips, sports, beliefs and even your religion may also be important. Of course, the model you make will be extremely individual.

Begin by weighting the connections according to their potential influence. Then use gradients (e.g., of yellow) or quantitative attributes (e.g. for the current state) for the factors that indicate integration; green for the factors that indicate development; and blue for the factors that indicate both. The gradients or attributes will help you to show whether you are currently feeling integrated and/or that you are developing, e.g., a light color if you have not achieved this feeling yet; a middle shade if you feel (or have started to feel) that from time to time, and a dark shade if you feel that you have achieved it fully. In the Insight Matrix you will then be able to see whether integration and development are balanced in your life.

Just having goals, however, does not suffice as a plan. You also need to identify measures that will help you to achieve your goals and also the obstacles that hinder you from being happy. You should therefore use the KNOW WHY Method here, too, and ask yourself what every factor needs and what might hinder one or the other until you can identify a concrete action for each goal you have in your life. Many aspects of your life are interdependent – especially if they require money and/or time. You can opt to either explicitly model time or money each as individual factors or let the factors directly influence each other.

I suggest you use, for example, orange for the actions that should or need to still be taken and red for the obstacles you identified. You can use light color gradients for actions that have been taken and which you were satisfied with or potential obstacles that only have a slight chance of having an impact, middle color gradients for actions and/or obstacles that have begun to have an effect or obstacles that are starting to pose a problem, and dark color gradients for actions you have planned but not yet implemented and problems that have started taking full effect.

It is also advisable to refresh your color gradients or attributes and the entire model from time to time. By doing so, you broaden your consciousness. You can have a HIDP for your life as a whole and HIDPs for every new year or even for shorter time periods. Whenever you feel lost have a look at your HIDP and see what actions you should be taking. Very often we lack the energy, the discipline and do not get the rewarding feeling we expect from these actions. So we postpone these actions and find ourselves trapped in a vicious circle. And we feel desperate. Thus we should add smaller actions/measures to our model, which we can implement immediately and which will give us the energy that comes with the feeling of success.

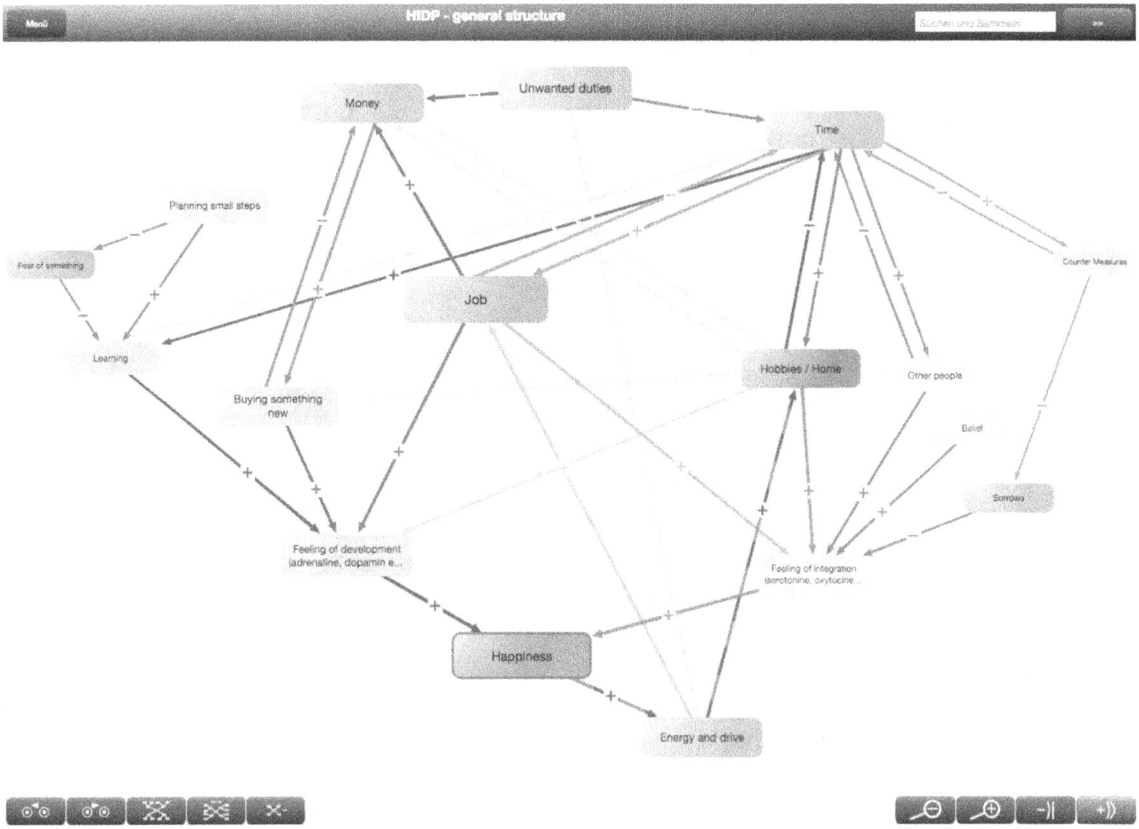

A general structure of a HIDP with time and money as explicit factors.

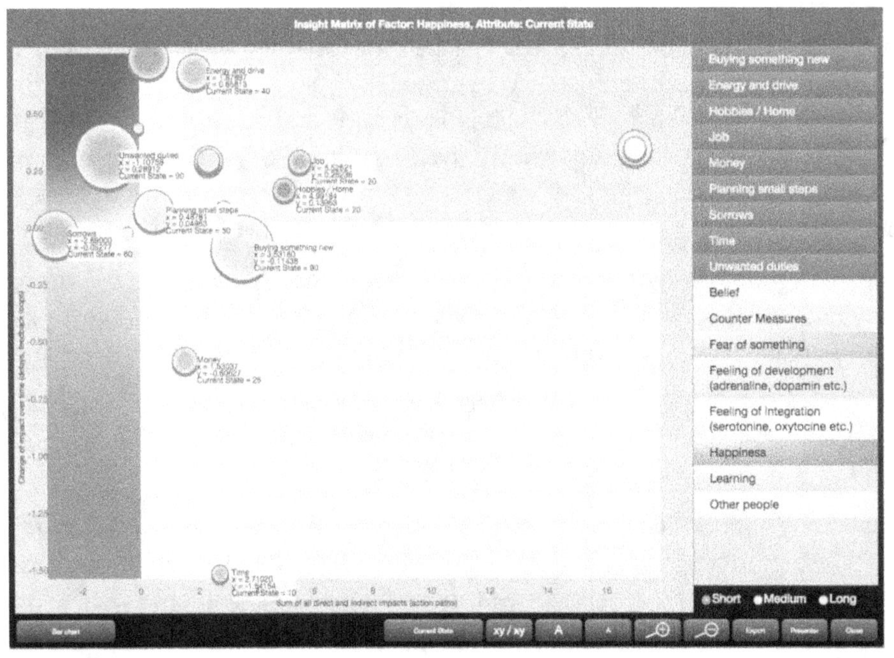

Colors or attributes (different diameter of factors) indicate if an action still needs to be implemented or a target still needs to be reached.

11. Helping and motivating people: coaching, NLP etc.

The HIDP is there to help you achieve personal happiness. Of course, you can synchronize your HIDP with your partner's and even with your entire family's HIDP. You can also help others to develop their own HIDP. This is the most effective kind of coaching – regardless of whether you are a soccer coach, a case manager or a grandpa. Not a single personal challenge exists that cannot either be linked back to a lack of integration or a lack of development. Thus you can reflect on every challenge using the KNOW WHY Thinking. Successful therapy and coaching sessions (NLP, body and mind management, etc.) work because they provide people with integrated development. Anchoring, reframing, etc. are techniques that only work if they result in a feeling of integration and/or development. However, quite often they also do not work at all, and, unfortunately, few therapists and NLP masters are familiar with KNOW WHY Thinking.

Interesting, too, is the fact that once people become acquainted with KNOW WHY Thinking, you'll see otherwise "rational" people trying out body and mind management techniques, for example, which they previously were not susceptible to. You might stop telling your clients, for instance, that relaxation, transcendence, etc. is good for them. Instead you say that according to evolutionary logic, everyone in general needs these things, and that it is possible but not a given that a certain approach, exercise, therapy, etc. will work. If you want to change someone's behavior – whether it is because they associate with the wrong crowd, waste their time away sitting passively in front of the TV or their computer, take drugs, misbehave, harm the environment or whatever – begin by asking yourself WHY they do it. What feeling might they get through their behavior? Then think of alternatives to their behavior that would give them feelings of integration and/or development. Whether these alternatives work or not is hard to predict, but without alternatives it is a sure thing that nothing will change. If you expect someone to be disciplined enough to do or abstain from doing certain things, keep in mind that it takes energy – energy that comes from feeling integrated and/or that one is developing. The "discipline muscle" needs to be trained.

If you want to increase motivation in your employees, children, friends or in your partner, you can model a HIDP with them. You can also, of course, model their HIDP alone for your own personal use, as you can benefit from knowing what could result in integration and/or development in their life. Your level of empathy will rise, the conversations you have with each other will become more meaningful, and you can make concrete suggestions on how they can improve their lives. In the best possible sense of the word, you can even use the knowledge you gain to manipulate them.

Can your employees feel integration and development in their jobs? Do they have a certain degree of freedom so that they can develop, value integration and have a nice place to feel integration? Change management and organizational development are fairly easy using KNOW WHY Thinking.

I have one important warning, however! When people sit down and model their HIDP, some may discover that they simply have no integration and/or development in their lives. If they are depressed by this, it will be your responsibility to motivate and stabilize them!

Systems archetype of psychological reactance and self-taught helplessness both figure in a virtuous circle of learning and self-esteem (integration and development), or in a vicious circle of not trying, not learning and decreasing self-esteem (no development, increasingly less integration).

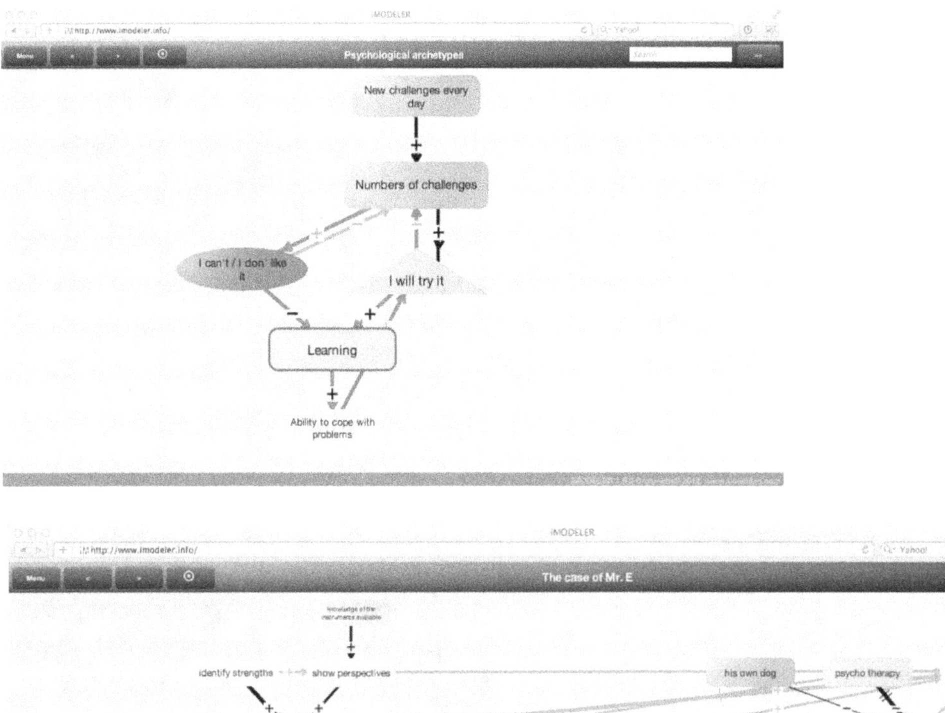

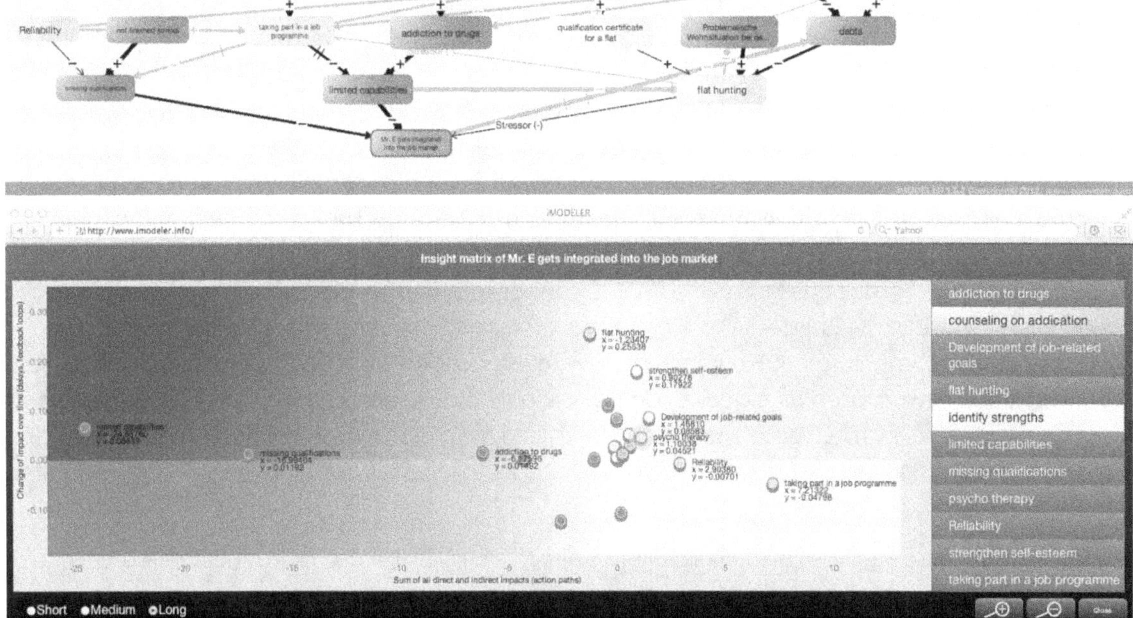

A model of a case manager reflecting on a client's situation. A case manager has to find out whether a client feels integration and development, and whether the suggested measures will result in too much development (case manager Susanne E. Bursch allowed me to use this anonymous case that can also be found on KNOW-WHY.NET).

12.   The KNOW WHY of business success

All companies need to "integrate and develop" in order to be successful. If they make a profit it is due to their integrated development; if they do not, it is because it is lacking. Many companies go about their business without much thought, or they copy the business plans of others; sometimes they even simply do what their CEO's gut feeling says they should. But in order to be successful most companies need to develop a strategy. This strategy may be in response to changing circumstances at a given point in time, or to implement a plan that will help the company to fulfill a set of missions and thus develop up towards the top of the wave and achieve its vision. A company's vision integrates its mission and the mission integrates the strategies, which include all processes and projects. These, as well as all of the resources employed, need to be planned and integrated into the overall organization of the company. Also, the leadership, the vision and the mission of a company provide the integration for the organization and its resources. Everything I have listed here develops what it is integrated by: the resources, too, serve to make the organization of a company develop. The organization makes it possible to develop processes and projects, which determine what strategies are needed if conditions change – conditions that threaten integration. Having a vision makes a company active instead of reactive. It also makes a company immune to crisis. But even without a vision or a mission, when a company only integrates itself through market demand it needs to develop strategies so that it can react and reintegrate when circumstances change.

Using the Know Why Method it is fairly simple to model a company as a whole (taking its purpose and systemic functioning into account). At first glance the approach might seem quite similar to that used for a balanced scorecard (BSC) or a dynamic strategy map. However, there is one important difference: using KNOW WHY makes it possible to really describe a company by including all of the influencing factors – everything from soft factors such as motivation, joy, honesty, transparency to particular events such as the threat of market turbulences or a change of technology to hard factors such as quality issues, loss of market share, etc. Most strategy development efforts are limited to a small set of factors that represent measurable scorecards. They don't help you understand the company, and for the employees the strategy means unrealistic, nonintegrated development. Unfortunately, many consultants lack the competence necessary to model the operations of a company. It is easier for them to simply take a given set of scorecards and determine that they describe the company. In some cases the companies have even needed to adapt to the scorecards! However, even if you have chosen to model a company and its operations as a whole, it is reasonable to identify measurable factors (each measure should lead to one) that drive the company. You can even use the four dimensions (financial, customer, internal processes, learning and growth) of a standard balanced scorecard.

Another popular approach to achieving business success is the use of business intelligence. Up until now, however, I feel that BI has been everything but intelligent. It simply means that you can generate flexible reports and gain a certain amount of data to support your limited reflection of the company. However, correlation does not imply causation. A model, in contrast, helps you to reflect, and the Insight Matrix can provide you with the necessary insights, showing you what the most effective measures are and also what risks you need to be wary of.

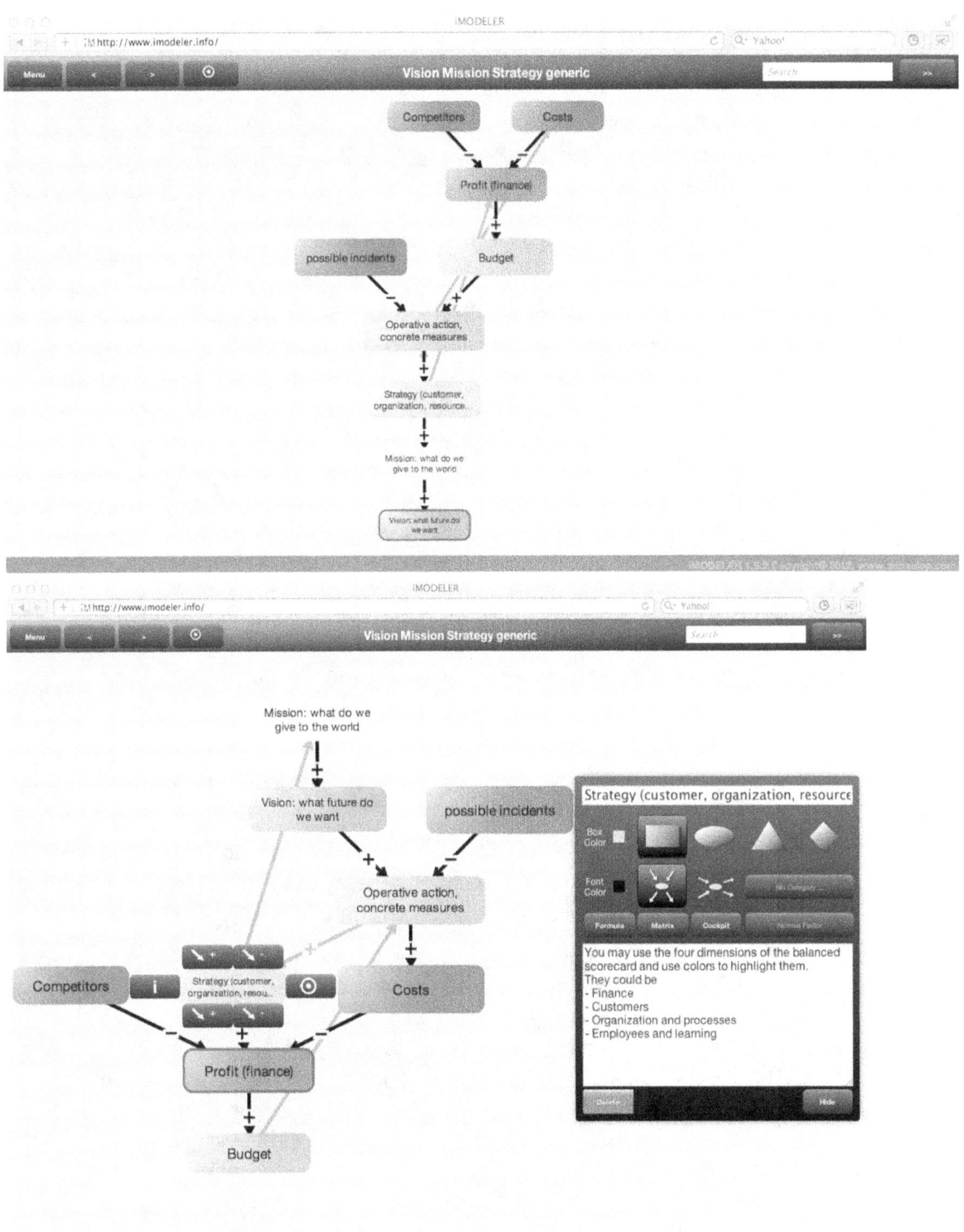

General structure of a strategy model. You should begin with the vision. Profit, if it is not already a strategic goal, will be included automatically as you will need a budget for operative measures.

13. Idealized System Design

If you are looking for a new solution, product, or invention – for everything from product development to your own personal life – then you have two choices. You can either continue developing the solutions that you are using today or you can find solutions for the future and ways to implement them today. The latter can be done using the KNOW WHY Method. I call it "Idealized Systems Design" (only later I have learned of Russell Ackhoff's Idealized Design and it is funny how similar the concept and the name are) and have found that the solutions obtained this way are nearly always superior to those obtained by simply continuing to develop your current solutions.

You can begin by either opting for a "science fiction" solution right away or after some reflection on the general properties your solution should have. A so-called science fiction solution is one that is totally unrealistic and yet provides your customers with the very best solution.

Taking this science fiction solution as a factor, you use the KNOW WHY Method and ask yourself what is needed to implement it and what might hinder it, both now and in the future. Of course, what is needed to implement it today will very likely be quite unrealistic. You may be required to defy gravity, have endless amounts of energy, be able to read people's minds or change their way of thinking, or even possess some indestructible material.

But if you proceed anyway and ask what the pertinent factors need and what their obstacles might be, then you will start thinking of ways that will make the solution feasible. Maybe you can find some good alternatives that bring you closer to your original solution. Or maybe you can find a couple of completely different (but feasible characteristics) for an alternative solution. You can later place an unnamed factor for an alternative solution next to the factor for the original science fiction solution.

In the end, your solution will either be your original science fiction solution, an altered version of it, an alternative very similar to it, or something completely new.

As you go through this process, you begin with the best solution you can think of and continue until you reach a solution that is possible to implement. This means that you go directly to the top of the wave instead of continuously improving on the solutions you use today "the wave up".

Apple, for example, supposedly does this. The company is not merely using the technology that is available today, but rather finds the best solution for their customers and then determines how it can be realized using today's technology. I doubt that Apple uses Idealized Systems Design as a technique, but I am also of the opinion that Apple has yet to present us with the very best solutions. The CONSIDEO iMODELER is the result of Idealized System Design. While the classic MODELER is an improvement of its predecessors, the iMODELER is an entirely new development. It has its roots in "science fiction solutions" and was conceived with the aim of working like the human brain. The roadmap of the iMODELER's development will have some surprises that probably will have little to do with the solutions we use today. For example the magic button to ask KNOW-WHY.NET works as if you sit in a room with numerous experts who look at their models and make proposals. The iMODELER's virtual collaboration space (coming soon) works as if you were sitting together with others in a room with each one having a computer in front of her or him with the possibility of letting the others looking at their screen.

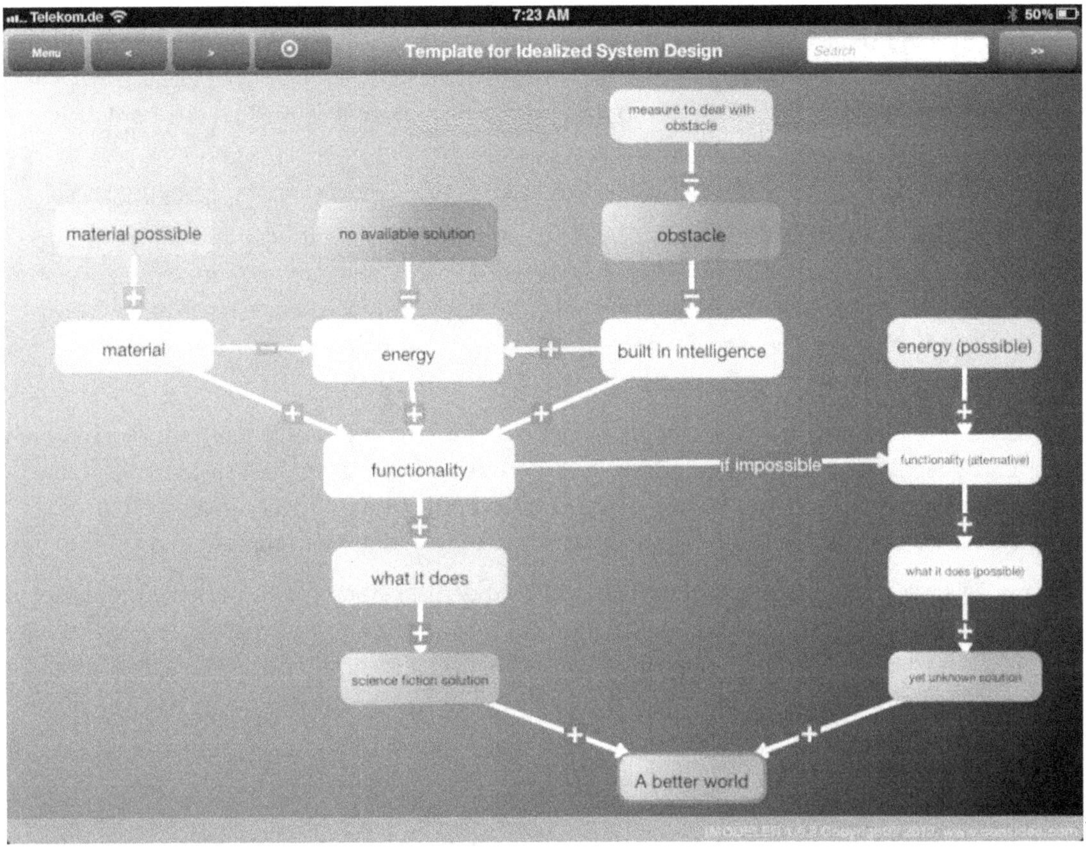

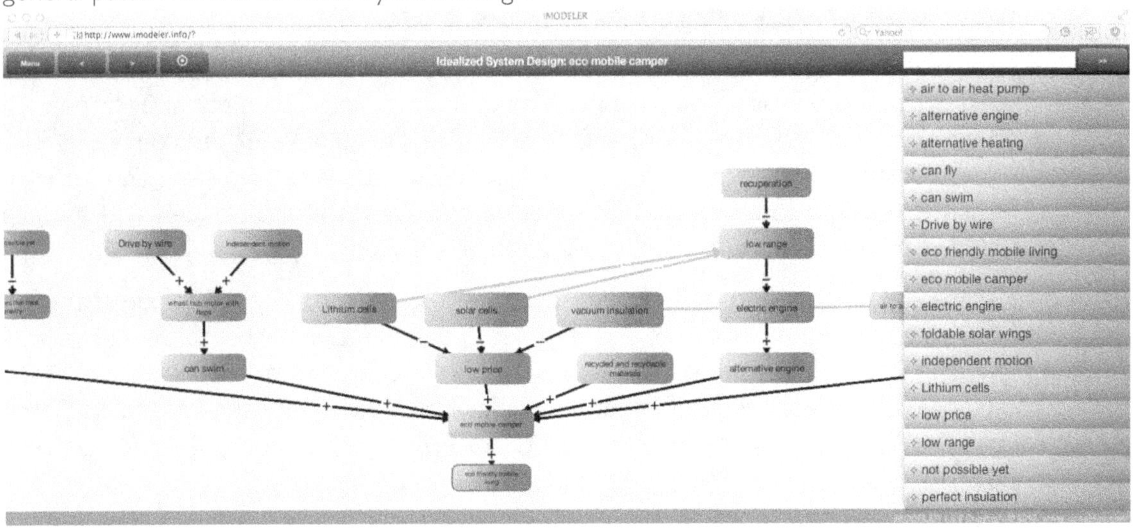

The general pattern of the Idealized System Design.

Starting a model to the invention of a new ecological camper.

14. Reflecting on processes and projects

Reflecting on processes and projects is something we do daily in our business lives. Most of us do this accompanied by strenuous thoughts or while in endless meetings. Some people use a variety of tools and concepts for project and process management such as Six Sigma, total quality management, lean management, etc. If those approaches fail, however, it is due to the complexity of the large number of factors involved that need to be considered.

Reflecting on processes is similar to that of reflecting on projects – and it is fairly simple: you can start with a goal and ask the KNOW WHY questions to implicitly get a chain of processes or project steps, or you can start by connecting the steps you already know are necessary and then continue on to ask about the integration and development involved in each step following the KNOW WHY Method. You add resources, incidents, requirements, measures, etc. as factors that serve to integrate or develop each step of the process or project.

The result is a reflection on what the management, the employees and the customers know using natural language without complicated business process modeling notations. This transparency integrates everybody involved. Modeling motivates, everybody is heard, ideally even the customer. Motivation is crucial and can be reached through transparency and good communication.

For a qualitative model, it is important that you connect the steps of the project or process with a weighting of 100 percent. Only then will the Insight Matrix of the factor that represents the ultimate goal at the end of the process or project correctly show just how important all the other factors along the chain are.

The weighting for the other connections shows how important a given factor is and what effect it has or would have. With color coding and gradients of a color or through a factor's quantitative attributes you can depict whether a risk is likely, a measure or a step has started or has been completed, or whether a goal has more or less been reached. This allows you to easily monitor the risks and progress of your project within the Insight Matrix.

Of course, many managers want concrete figures and hence a quantitative model that simulates a bandwidth of possible scenarios that take the likelihood of risks into account. Making a linear simulation (as can be done with other tools) is fairly simple. In reality, however, the complexity involved stems from nonlinear developments, from interdependencies between the steps and from the resources and external factors. They can be modeled, too. They can also be identified through the KNOW WHY Method and the possible impacts can be analyzed through the simulations.

However, the formulas to describe how one step depends on the capacity of resources that remain from other steps that have a higher priority can become very elaborate. For this challenge we offer the PROCESS iMODELER feature, which allows you to include special factors that represent resources, processes and milestones. The result is a simulation that shows the constraints (theory of constraints, ToC), points in time where resources are fully engaged and limit a given process and where the stocks available indicate these bottlenecks.

Reflecting on projects also results in profound qualitative and quantitative risk and portfolio management.

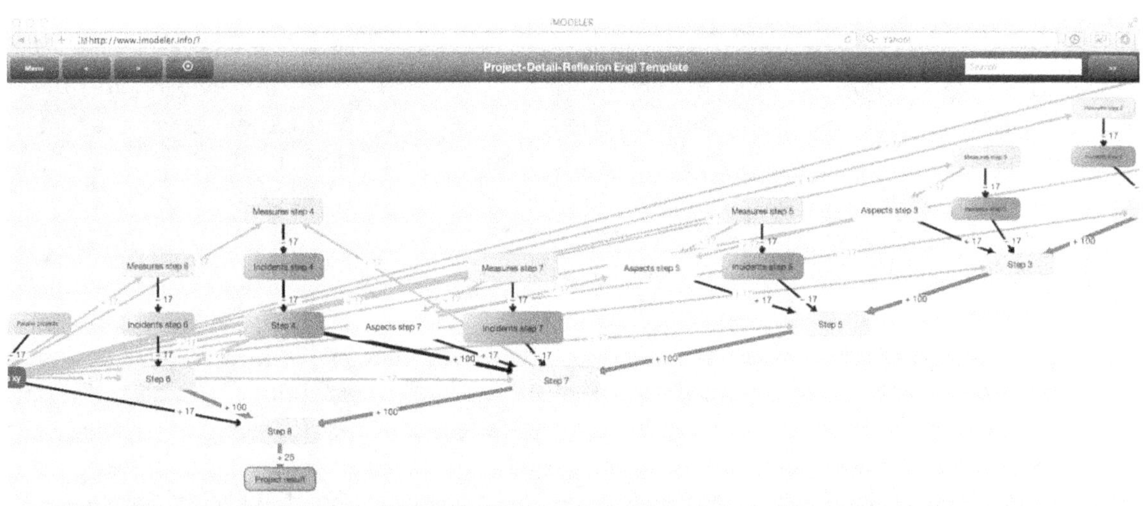

The steps of a project or process connected to each other with a weighting of 100 percent. The crucial impacts are identified with the KNOW WHY Method. The colors (alternatively to quantitative attributes) indicate the likelihood of a risk and the current state of a project/process step.

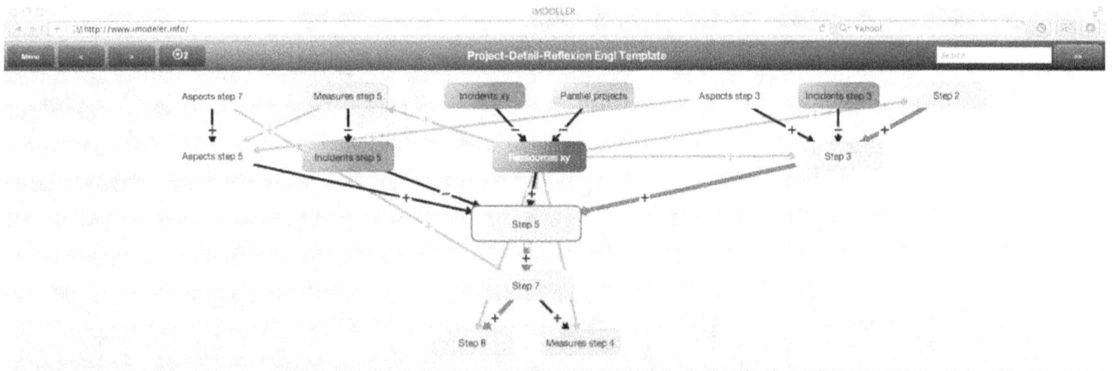

No matter how large the process is each step from its perspective remains concise.

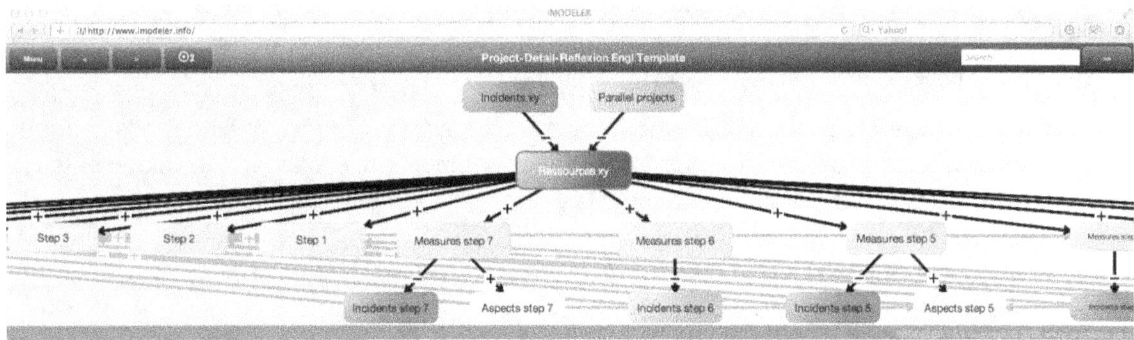

The perspective of every resource clearly shows its connections. For more have a look at examples on KNOW-WHY.NET

15.   The KNOW-WHY of successful marketing

Whether a product is successful or not depends on its benefit to the customer. Either the customer needs it or the customer wants it. And even if the customer needs it, it is possible to make them connect with it emotionally and choose it over a competitor's product. The product, the service, the marketing and even the corporate identity provided by the creator of a product need to give the customer a feeling of integration and/or development. We can reflect explicitly on this while developing products, marketing them, selling them and providing services for them. However, we are not always required to model this. We often just need to ask ourselves if a product offers the customers too much or not enough development.

A product can make a customer feel good, maybe even become a kind of daily companion. It should have a striking name, making it pleasant to think and speak about. This is part of its integration. However, if the target customer is looking for a feeling of development, the product needs to have new features and work differently than products that came before it. At any rate, a product needs to have a unique selling point (USP). It is frustrating how often the USP of products and services cannot be identified. The communication and the marketing of a product must have a message, a unique selling point, a memorable phrase or slogan associated with it as well as several effective channels for its promotion. Some advertising works through mere repetition, but there is also advertising that works through effective bisociation, which integrates a theme and develops it with an either emotional or cognitive surprise for the customer.

The Holy Grail of marketing is the word-of-mouth effect. To reach a tipping point (M. Gladwell) where your product sells without your help it needs a message, people who are connected and who will feel integration by telling others about the message, and, of course, a product that does not exhibit too much but rather just enough development. This may sound trivial but is provides astonishing insights into the integration and development of a message, a communication channel and the product itself. I think – therefore iM!

In most cases it is worth modeling the marketing management of a company. In a qualitative model you can continue with the strategic model or start a new model, where the profit from a product or a portfolio of products is your central factor. The profit depends on the sales, the price and your expenses. The sales depend on the rational and emotional benefit that the product has to the customer and whether the customer even knows about the product and can purchase it. Whether a product is known depends on the channels and the message that also decides whether a customer wants the product. The message depends on the product features.

According to the KNOW WHY Method, you must always ask what might hinder a factor and what will be important in the future. Thus you consider competitors, economical developments and the life cycle of the product. A quantified model facilitates corporate foresights.

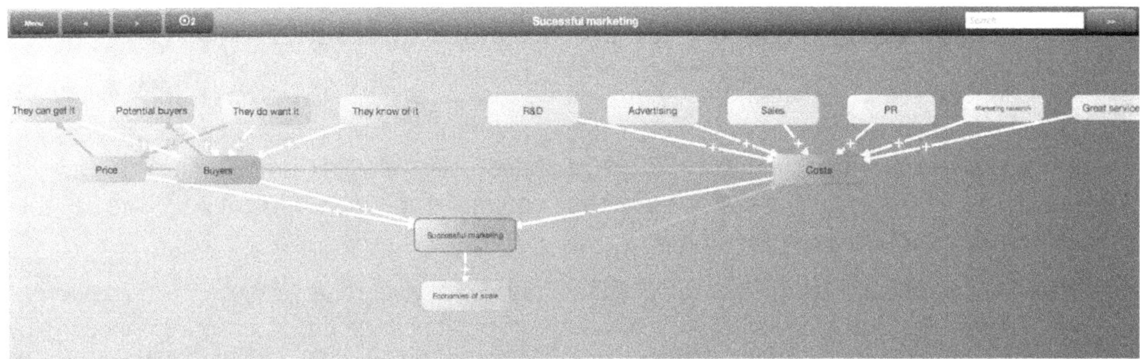

The first two levels of a general model on successful marketing.

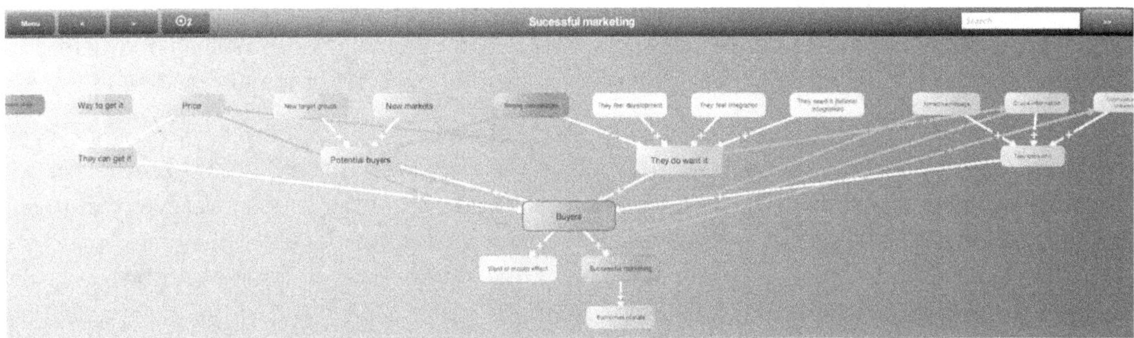

The success of marketing depends on the possibility of the customer feeling integration and/or development or his or her rational integration and/or development.

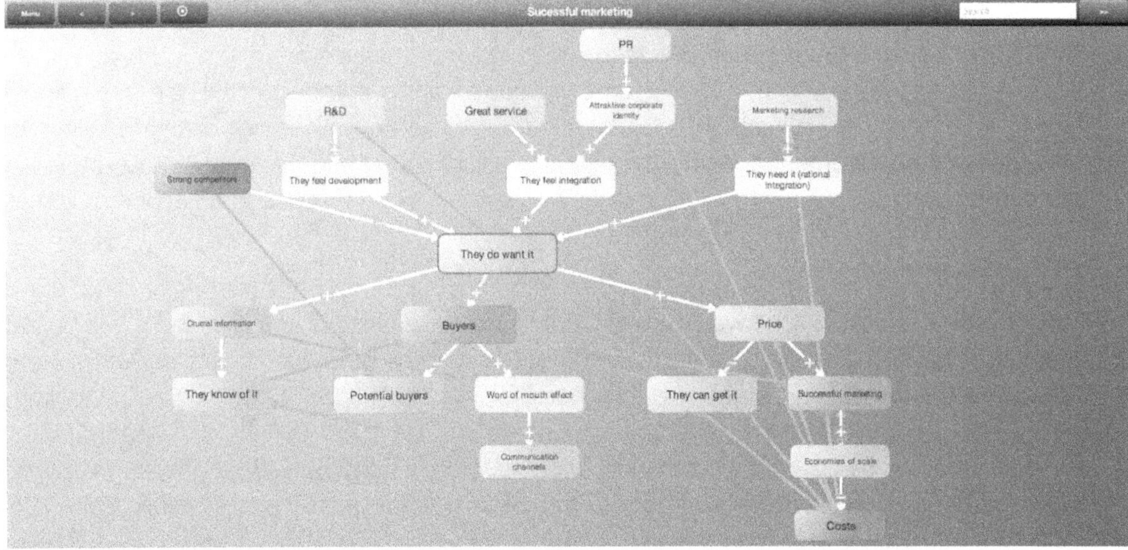

The activities for marketing need to cause a feeling of integration and/or development

16. Our history: merely an unfortunate accident?

The development of humankind and civilization is truly amazing. Some say it is God's will, while others say that all development is the logical consequence of a large number of circumstances we cannot influence. I fear that already the next generation will view our historical heritage as a logical consequence of the dynamics of our quest for integration and development. And one day, they will tell us how we jeopardized their future.

Wars are no longer fought simply for survival. I think that everyone will agree with me when I say that it should be possible today to prevent wars through economical and political sanctions, by doing away with the arms trade and weapons and that people should be able to feel integrated without the existence of war and the need for an enemy. To understand why wars happen we need to reflect on the reasons why some countries don't want to impose sanctions, why there is arms trade, why people out of despair, grinding poverty and injustice choose religion and demagoguery. The development of wars and weapons goes far beyond the crest of the KNOW WHY Wave.

Religion prevents rational logic and in some states of the US up until this very day it is still an implicit tool used by certain powerful people to attain their maximum benefit since it prevents important changes. It is election year (2013) in the US and a large part of the country believes that the nation doesn't need to change. This is because God has told two candidates that they must make the US as powerful as it once was by lowering taxes for the rich (causing inequality) and by exploiting natural resources (causing environmental pollution). It used to be the case that our belief in God helped to ensure that we felt integrated because our religion told us why things were the way they were. We by no means are able to explain everything in the world today, but we do know that many things certainly are not God's will, but rather the will of demagogues.

Each country has its share of poverty, but developing countries have more poverty than most. Interestingly enough we want everyone to strive to attain the same amount of wealth so that we can sell our products. And yet at the same time we don't want everyone to have the same amount of wealth as we do. Cars, gadgets, skyscrapers, leisure trips and even our rich diets are all because of our quest for development, which is the logical result of having and being more than others. Apart from the moral aspects of why there should be more equality, there is also an economical side that I will address in the next few chapters.

Pollution, climate change and the depletion of resources is another embarrassing result of our history. Many people believe that we have started to change our habits and that there will be enough time for us to adapt to changes and that we really have no choice. I, too, drive a car and can think of reasons as to why I believe that there is no need for me to change. Maybe it is already too late, but for sure our civilization will fail if there is not a radical change in our definition of wealth; if there are no strong politics based on enlightenment and provided by opinion leaders, the media and education combined with role models who show us how to feel integration and development in a different - as it is exchangeable - way.

At the end of the day, it is all simply because we want or have to feel integration and development and because we lack reason and morals due to our lack of awareness. I model – therefore iM!

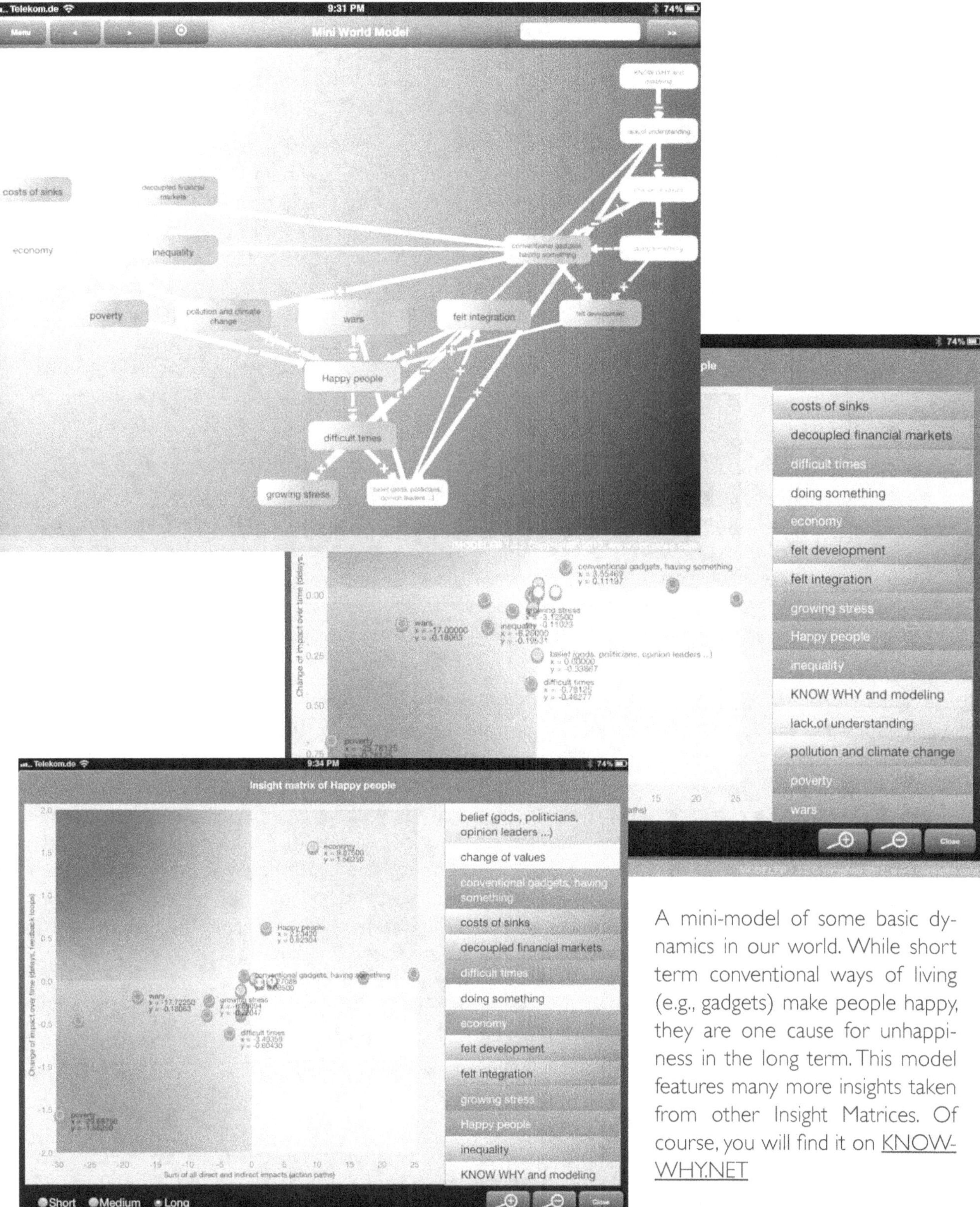

A mini-model of some basic dynamics in our world. While short term conventional ways of living (e.g., gadgets) make people happy, they are one cause for unhappiness in the long term. This model features many more insights taken from other Insight Matrices. Of course, you will find it on KNOW-WHY.NET

17. The global economy: a closed loop

The economy is very simple. People offer things and services that are in demand in exchange for money so that they too have the means to purchase what other people are offering. How much we all can get from this system depends on productivity.

The stagnation of productivity in this system leads to a state of equilibrium. But there is some variance in the game, since there is inequality. Some people have to work more for their money than others do. And those who work less yet can produce more can then easily beat out competitors and make a surplus. They can loan this money to others who can use it to start companies, projects or other endeavors. If they don't loan out this money, however, other people won't be able to purchase their products and hence they threaten their own future income. If their interest rate is too high others will have less money to spend and the lenders will gain ever more. Inequality will inevitably rise. There will, however, come a point where borrowers pay so much interests that they cannot be productive anymore and nor can they purchase from lenders. They will loose all their possessions.

If other people in addition to this receive loans for consumption, the lenders will end up owning even more – this is a result of reinforcing feedback loops. Unless these people start earning a higher income, they will become poorer on account of the interest rates. They get higher incomes not solely because of their productivity but because of the growth of the market volume in other markets and because of inflation caused by that growth and the increase of credit volume. The credit volume is defined by regulations that continuously change: ever less money or gold needs to be physically available for banks to lend money. Banks are allowed to earn interests on money that doesn't exist.

So far so good. A system could still be stable and healthy under these conditions. However, instead of reinvesting this money into the real economy through loans, more and more wealthy people and institutions are investing in what I call "creative financial products." They make money in the real economy and try to maximize their profits apart from the real economy. The money is therefore missing in the real economy and the only benefit that the creative financial products have is that they hide the troublesome total amount of debt. Today the volume of the financial markets is 65 times higher than that of the real economy. This is definitely too much development without integration. The entire system depends on growth because it depends on loans for investments as well as for consumption. Today we bail out the financial system to help the real economy, but as long as creative financial products are still permitted, everyone (especially in times of crisis) will do everything to maximize their profits on the financial markets and not in the real economy. Simply put and to reiterate: we can only earn what others spend. And they can only spend what they earn because we buy what they offer. Everyone with an above average income has this income because of the many people that earn a below average income. The amount of money on the market should be coupled to the rise of productivity. At some point in the future it could mean that we all need to work less. Finally, without interests and competition there is no progress. What we therefore need to do is to integrate our development through stricter regulations that must stem from international politics. The system we have today will soon collapse. I will address this point in more depth in the next two chapters.

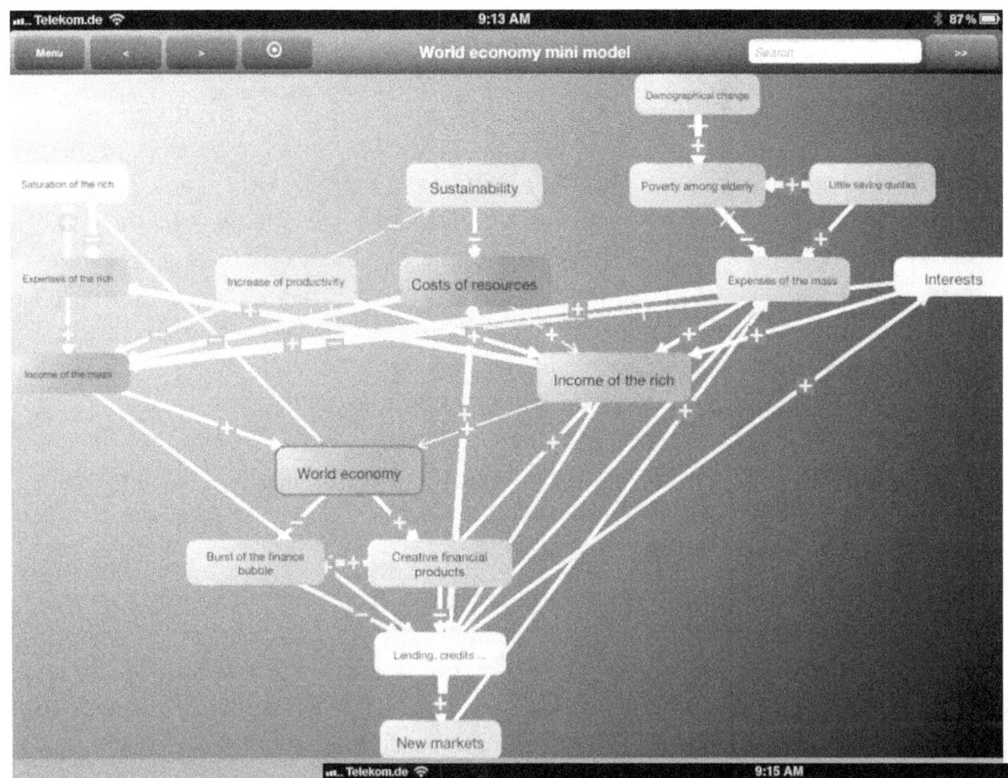

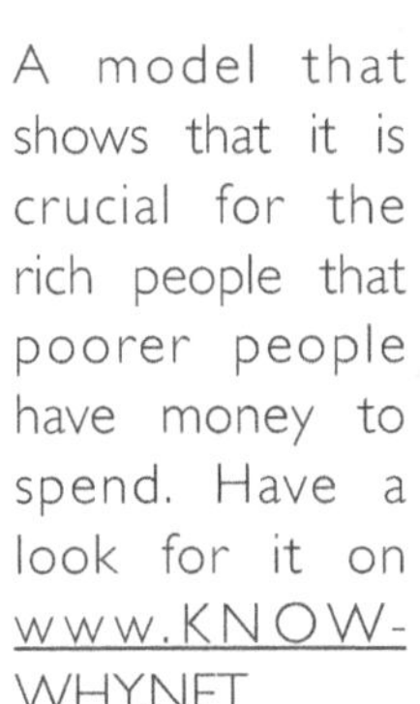

A model that shows that it is crucial for the rich people that poorer people have money to spend. Have a look for it on www.KNOW-WHY.NET

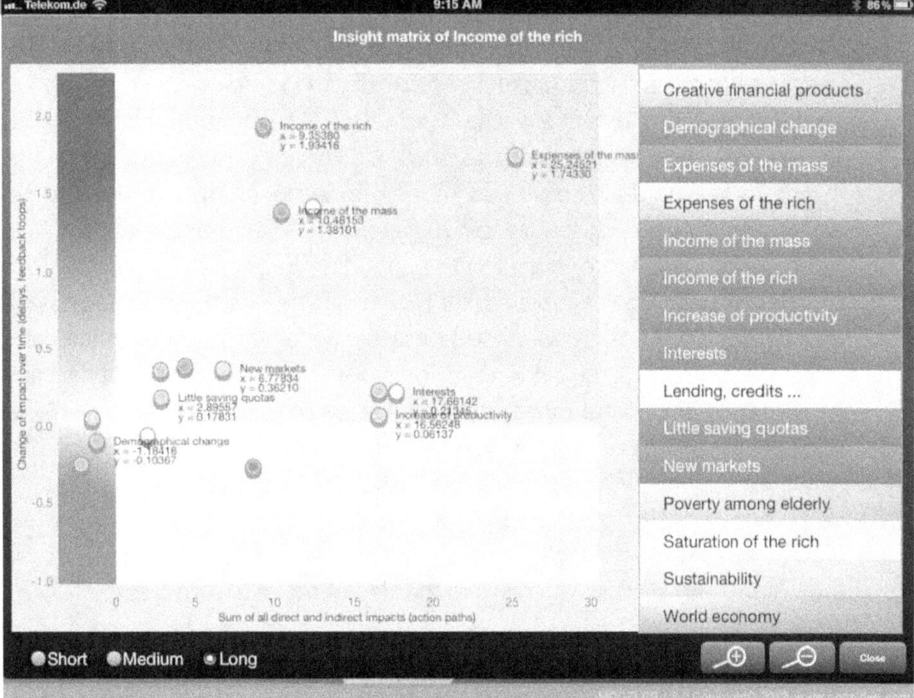

18.   Sustainability: a concerted action

For many people, the idea of sustainability and of protecting the environment is a rather romantic one that can only be realized to the extent that it does not restrict the maximum benefits we reap from our high standard of living today and our economical activities. In other words: if an electric car offers us the same performance for the same price as a conventional car does, we go for it. If it does not, however, we wait until we are forced to purchase one or others do so, leading the way. The problem with environmental damage is that the Earth and its organisms can take so much. The damages are not dramatic enough: polluted oceans, the hole in the ozone layer and even acid soil all seem to recover eventually. Even if there is only 70 percent of the ocean's fish left, the good news is that many stocks grow again. So let us continue fishing. There is radioactivity in our drinking water and there are harmful chemicals in animals and in our children's tissue? They won't die from it, so let's increase the permissible levels. In order for people to change from insights, damages seem to need to be more dramatic, the way that the nuclear catastrophe in Fukushima was. Even the rising costs associated with natural disasters are not felt.

Sustainability is not just about minimizing environmental damage or a question of whether the following generations will need to find a way to live without the resources we continue to waste today. Already now dwindling resources are a severe threat to our economic system. We will be on the brink of catastrophe when only a small price increase for key resources paired with some bad news triggers a chain reaction on the markets. The economy is based on psychology to a very high degree. Companies invest when they have confidence in the markets; consumers take out loans for consumption; and banks lend out money. If at one point this engine stops, the entire system may very well come to a grinding halt within days. And no, there is not enough money that people will spend anyway because there is less money in circulation than debt owned. So with the depletion of key resources it is only logical that they will end up costing more. And the increased cost of obtaining them will naturally leave less money for other things we need or want! The car industry, real estate, the service industry, gadget makers, etc., will all earn less money. Unemployment will rise and people's fear will cause them to stop spending. Exports to resource-rich countries will not be able to compensate for this development because they will have already started their own competitive industries, which are growing. And because we already made additional money available when the last crisis hit, such a measure is no longer an option. Sustainability means preventing sinks, non-renewable resources and money that cannot be regained. We have to close material cycles, reuse and recycle or simply prevent the need for resources. A change won't come about from mere insights, however, and we will insist that our quality of living remain high – that we feel integration and development. We will have to follow a different set of criteria or apply the same criteria in a different way. To invest in sustainable solutions fosters the economy. To wait just makes those solutions more expensive with the rise of costs for the depleting fossil resources.

We need a clever and thus attractive system that we can use to measure our ecological footprint from the things we buy, the things we do and also the things that we don't buy and don't do! Such a system will lead to our products becoming more intelligent and our values will change, too. Achieving such a system, opinion leaders, the media and even politics will integrate change through the transparency of the interconnections. Our economy will probably flourish because of it.

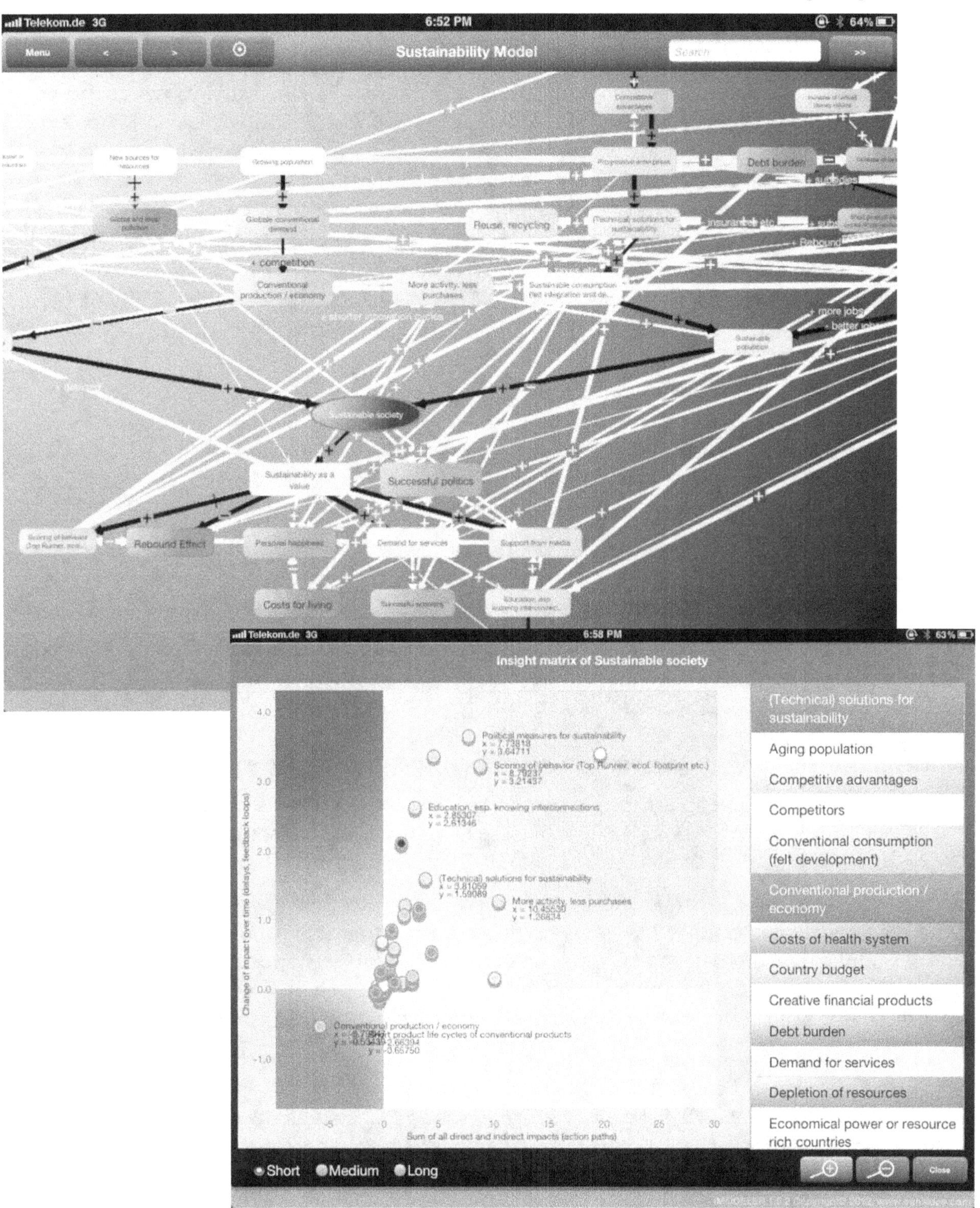

A model of sustainability showing what a mighty lever scoring our behavior would be

19. Global spirit and global politics

To reduce poverty, save the environment, prevent climate change, wars and terrorism, and to be prepared for the upcoming collapse of the financial system, we need to internationalize politics. Politics today is defined more by people trying to gain power than by people who want to take responsibility for our world. They fight for a few people's interests and yet sell this as many people's interests. Everything they do is only for their term in office. All regions and countries stand in competition with each other as if they were companies with products on offer. The same can almost be said for individuals as well. We only change or develop if others change, too, because otherwise the change would not be integrated development, meaning that we would fall off of the KNOW WHY Wave. Politicians won't be elected, products won't be sold and our way of living won't find acceptance or even be admired.

Before a sustainable politics, product or service is delivered, people first have to know that it is in demand, so that they can offer it. But people who know what should be in demand cannot understand why things don't change. I know this and I also know how we all need to change – and yet I still take long hot showers and drive a car. If people who are intelligent enough to know that change is necessary don't change then how can we expect all the others to change?

We can wait for catastrophes to happen, for financial collapse, for terror with dirty nuclear bombs, rising sea levels, etc., or we can integrate the change through transparent interconnections and develop through a system that measures a better way of life.

Conservative thinking and politics prevent the change that we need from happening. We also need to share a language, probably English, and we need to make religion a matter of taste and not truth. We need to internationalize politics without making it Western politics. The UN shouldn't be located in the US and decisions should be made with equal input and not just at G7 meetings. We need international education, exchange students, more sports and more women empowerment.

With more international politics, we can start to ban the production of weapons. They are an unintelligent sink anyway. We need to tax sinks, the use of resources that cannot be reused. We need to control the financial markets and restart with an integrated system.

Instead of weapons and armies we must intervene and protect the environment. Of course, a whole industry of lobbyists will try everything to prevent us from doing this, but at least the same amount of jobs and profits can be gained through the alternatives, with the only difference being that they are no sinks. Also we need open markets to develop a healthy economical system of a real economy with profits, loans and an increase of productivity.

To achieve political change we need smart people that people believe in. Belief is something we fall back on when we find ourselves having a difficult time understanding a situation. In desperate times it is just as likely that we will believe in a smart person as in a less smart person who promises us more. So smart people need to make promises to simple-minded people, too! This is the light and the dark side of the Force.

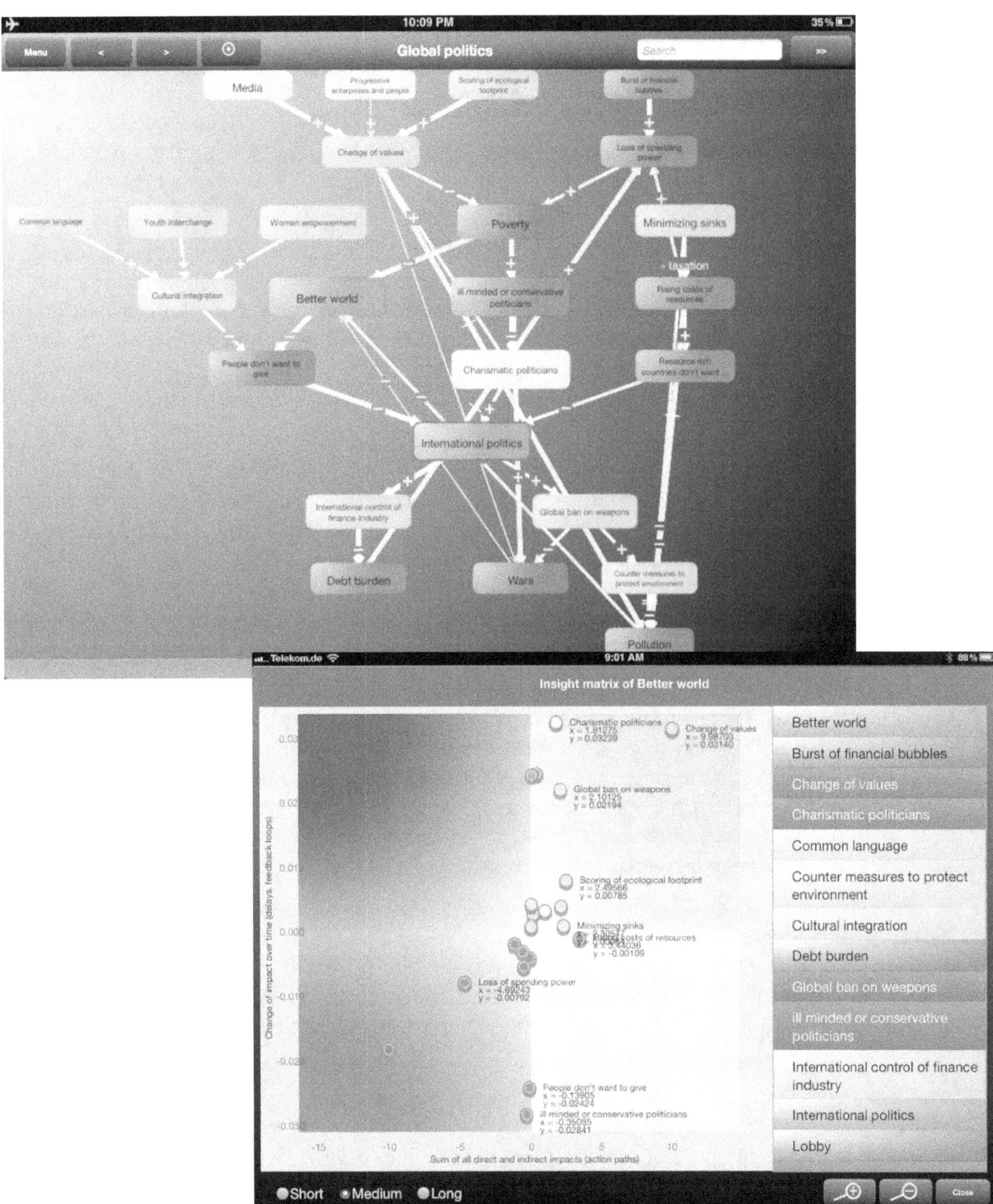

Model on global politics from <u>KNOW-WHY.NET</u>, showing the loss of spending power as the biggest threat and the change of values as the biggest lever.

20.   What can we do?

In the previous chapters I explained how everyone waits for others to take action before they, too, start making the world a better place. There is plenty of room in the world for progressive consumers, politicians, the media and companies who do all that they can to change the world. Although the measures that really need to be taken should be radical, at the same time they shouldn't be – because that in many cases could mean too much development without integration.

Although a smart system has yet to become available that allows us to measure our ecological footprint we can already start to reflect on this footprint now. Each and every one of us can make gradual lifestyle changes, on a yearly or even monthly basis. We can waste less, drive our cars less, use less water, start eating organic and wearing ecological clothing; we can turn off our air conditioning systems and heaters, etc. It won't be long before a system to score our ecological footprint shows us just how much good we are doing the environment, and we can share and compare our behavior with others, too.

Already now many companies and enterprises have started offering eco-friendly products. They need to be authentically ecological, however. Studies have shown that once consumers learn that an ecological product really was not ecological they will rebound and begin using the products they used before or go back to their old behavior There has already been a great deal of media attention surrounding sustainability and consumers have been given a great deal of background information about the interconnections involved. It seems that only politicians are lagging behind.

To improve your business, you can make reflection and modeling mandatory before decisions and plans are made. This will result in a new culture of planning, decision-making and communication. You will find yourself starting to act instead of just reacting. And the key to establishing the use of modeling in your business practices is to make sure that you always use natural language to describe interconnections and that you use the KNOW WHY Method to develop insightful models. Even if you don't have a smartphone or computer at hand, you can still reflect on the measures you want to implement by explicitly thinking about the integration and development of the factors involved – and their position on the KNOW WHY Wave.

To improve your personal life, you also simply need to reflect more often on more things in your life. Hang up an image of the KNOW WHY Wave in your bathroom, in your car or wherever you want to remind yourself that you need to reflect more. Make your HIDP and continuously work on it. It is as simple as that. You will soon feel and recognize that doing something is better than being someone and that having things will no longer be so important if you do things.

Not everyone can act as consciously as the average reader of this text can. Most people want to do what feels good, not what for rational reasons is good. Even people in high places prefer to follow their gut feeling and do what feels good. And they fear that they will feel less integrated if they have to admit that a solution does not come to them, but that they have to work at finding one, maybe even being required to ask for help. When you ask others for help, try to integrate them so that your request does not mean too much development for them.

Schoolchildren also need to be taught to reflect on things. They are taught how things come to be but not why. They don't learn to explore how things are interconnected. Instead, they are expected to simply accept that certain things are interconnected. We at CONSIDEO support schools and universities by providing the MODELER and the iMODELER free of charge for educational purposes.

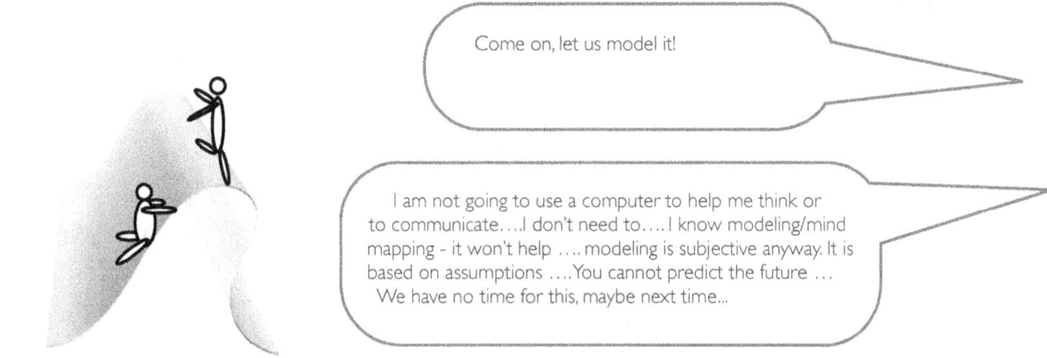

In many cases modeling means too much development for certain people. They aren't familiar with it, they fear transparency, they don't want to make the extra effort. Thus modeling sometimes need to be mandatory.

If a goal means too much development determine subgoals that will ensure it integrated development

Where on the wave is that what you are thinking about right now? Where are you on your wave today? Draw your waves or think of them ....

21.   KNOW WHY Thinking: a new science science and philosophy?

As I stated in chapter 3, KNOW WHY Thinking is a systems theory. Actually, it is a meta-systemic explanation of the success or failure of things that we can observe. It cannot tell us exactly what is needed for success, but it does describe what characteristics something needs to make it successful. Based on the evolutionary logic that everything needs to be integrated and develop, this information is quite fuzzy, but unlike other approaches, taking this one helps us to reflect on everything. We still need to use our brains, apply our knowledge, our intuition and our creativity – but unlike other systemic approaches it always provides an explanation.

We need philosophy if we cannot explain something scientifically – unless, of course, we choose to explain it as being God's will. Science offers explanations that seem to have been proven – in most cases by means of reproducible experiments, representative studies, or, as is the case in the social sciences, by means of the strange logic that results from citing a mix of references. It is indeed a bizarre notion that something should be true simply because a renowned person said it was without actually haven proven it is based on facts. And experiments, too, often only attain certain results under special, often idealized conditions. And just because a study is called representative, does it really mean that it is?

We need to distinguish between deductive, inductive and abductive logic. Deductive means that if the general case is true, then the specific one is true, too. However, there are actually only general cases in mathematics. We should never ;-) use all quantifiers such as 'always,' 'every,' 'never,' etc. Hence, everything ;-) is indeed inductive logic, which means that many cases are true, and therefore we just assume that there is a general rule to something until we can prove that something else is the case. We should always say that something is allegedly true and not that it is true for certain.

Language in and of itself isn't precise at all either. It is a convention. When we use language we hope that everybody means the same thing with the words they choose. However, what we actually connote with a word, what we perceive and what we mean, is subjective. In reality, we might very well be saying something completely different than what others perceive. Constructivism deals with this challenge. Abductive logic means that something would be true if there was a general rule. So we start by assuming this rule and then try to explain a given phenomenon by applying it. Modeling pure mathematics might be deductive logic, but in most cases, modeling is based on inductive logic, assuming that there are connections of a certain weight or that they can be described by a certain formula based on generally accepted knowledge, a decent number of observations or people's gut feeling. Nevertheless, it is quite often the case that we need to do some guesswork within a model to discover that which describes what we are able to observe. This is abductive logic, used in, e.g., Grounded Theory. Within the science society there is an ongoing dispute as to whether or not this is scientific. But how can we explore singularities or – even more importantly – future developments with unknown impacts caused by various factors if not through assumptions that can be validated over time and compared with different assumptions? We cannot explain the future solely based on the present, and so-called scientific proofs! A model is just a model, but it is a good start. It is the sensible thing to do and ought to be an accepted tool not just within the scientific community!

22. Useful Literature

Altshuller, Genrich: "And suddenly the inventor appeared: Triz, the Theory of Inventive Problem Solving"; 1996

Arpe, J., Glockner, H. et al: "Die ökonomischen Risiken der Globalisierung", 2012

Ashby, W. R.: „An introduction to cybernetics", 2012

Barber, Benjamin: "Consumed: How Markets Corrupt Children, Infantilize Adults, and Swallow Citizens Whole"; 2008

Bacon, Francis: "The essays"; 1620

Barber, Benjamin: "Consumed: How Markets Corrupt Children, Infantilize Adults, and Swallow Citizens Whole", 2008

Baumeister, R. F.; Tierney, J.: "Willpower"; 2011

Beck, D.E., Cowan C.C.: "Spiral Dynamics"; 2005

Beer, Stafford: "Brain of the firm"; 2005

Beinhocker, Eric D.: "The origin of wealth - the radical remaking of economics and what it means for business and society"; 2007

Binswanger: "Die Wachstumsspirale. Geld, Energie und Imagination in der Dynamik des Marktprozesses", 2006

Boden, Margaret A. (Ed.): "Dimensions of Creativity"; 1994

Bossel, Hartmut: "Systems and Models: Complexity, Dynamics, Evolution, Sustainability"; 2007

Bourdieu, Pierre: "Die feinen Unterschiede. Kritik der gesellschaftlichen Urteilskraft"; 1987

Brockman, John & Katinka: "How things are: A Science Toolkit for the Mind;" 1996

Brockman, J. (Hrsg): "The Mind: Leading Scientists Explore the Brain, Memory Personality and Happiness", 2011

Buchanan, Mark: "Ubiquity - why catastrophes happen"; 2000

Buzan, Tony: "Harnessing the Parabrain"; 1977

Capra, Fritjof: "The hidden connections;" 2003

Crouch, Colin: „The Strange Non-Death of Neoliberalism", 2011

Devitt & Sterelny: "Language and Reality"; 1987

Dispenza, Joe: "Evolve your Brain: The Science of Changing Your Mind", 2009

Dörner, Dietrich: "Die Logik des Misslingens" (English: The Logic of Failure: Recognizing and Avoiding Error in Complex Situations); 2003

Ekins, Paul: "Resource Productivity, Environmental Tax Reform and Sustainable Growth in Europe", 2009

Feldenkrais, Moshe: "Die Feldenkraismethode in Aktion"; 2006

Forgas, J.P. (Ed.): Psychology of Self-Regulation: Cognitive, Affective, and Motivational Processes; 2009

Forgas, J.P.: "Social Motivation: Conscious and Unconscious Processes"; 2009

Furuhashi, Takeshi et al. (Eds.): "Fuzzy Logic, Neural Networks, and Evolutionary Computation"; 1996

Gharajedaghi, Jamshid: "Systems Thinking – Managing Chaos and Complexity"; 2006

Gigerenzer, Gerd: "Bauchentscheidungen - Die Intelligenz des Unbewussten und die Macht der Intuition"; 2008

Gladwell, Malcolm: "The Tipping Point"; 1995

Gladwell, Malcolm: "Outliers - The story of success"; 2008

Gladwell, Malcolm: "Blink: The power of thinking without thinking"; 2006

Goldratt, E.M.: "Critical Chain"; 1997

Goleman, Daniel: "Emotional Intelligence"; 1995

Gorman, Philip: "Motivation and Emotion"; 2004

Ghoshal, S./Bartlett, C.A.: "The individualized corporation"; 1997

Gribbin , John: "Schrödingers Kittens - and the search for reality"; 1995

Halford, G.: "How many variables can humans process," Psychological Science, 16(1): 70-76., 2005

Hampden Turner, Charles: "Maps of the mind"; 1982

Howard, Godfrey: "Getting through"; 1989

Jackson, Michael: "Systems Approaches to Management"; 2000

Jackson, Tim: "Prosperity without growth - Economics for a finite planet", 2009

Jaynes, Julian: "The origin of consciousness in the breakdown of the bicameral mind"; 1976

Kahneman, Daniel: "Thinking, Fast and Slow"; 2012

Kaplan, Robert S.: "Strategy Maps"; 2004

Kasser, T.: "The high price of materialism", 2002

Koestler, Arthur: "Janus - A Summing Up", 1981

Kosko, Bart: "Fuzzy Cognitive Maps" International Journal Man-Machine Studies, p 65-75; 1985

Layard, Richard: "Happiness: Lessons from a New Science", 2011

Levitt,, Steven D., Dubner, Stephen J.: "Freakonomics"; 2005

Liker, J.K.: "The Toyota Way"; 2000

Lovelock, James: "The vanishing face of GAIA: A final warning;" 2009

Luhmann, Niklas: "Introduction to Systems Theory"; 2012

Maedows, D.H. & D, Randers, J.: "The Limits to Growth: The 30-Year Update"; 2007

Maturana, Humberto R.: "Tree of Knowledge: Biological Roots of Human Understanding"; 1992

MacHugh, P., Merli, G., Wheeler III, W.A.: "Beyond Business Process Reengineering Towards the Holonic Enterprise;" 1995

Maxwell, Joseph A.: "A Realist Approach for Qualitative Research", 2012

McNeill, Daniel, Freiberger, Paul: "Fuzzy Logic"; 1993

McClelland, David: "Human Motivation", 2009

Mitchell, Melanie: "Complexity: A guided tour"; 2009

Moore, Geoffrey A.: "Crossing the Chasm"; 2002

Morris, Desmond: "The human animal"; 1995

Neumann, K.: "KNOW WHY Thinking as a New Approach to Systems Thinking", in E:CO Issue Vol. 15 No. 3 2013 pp. 81-93 (ISSN: 1521-3259)

Neumann, K.: "KNOW WHY and the iMODELER" interactive eBook available only at the Apple iBook Store.

Neumann, K.; Grimm, F.; Heinrichs, H.: "Entwicklung eines Integrated Assessment Modells: Nachhaltige Entwicklung in Deutschland"; 2014 (http://www.umweltbundesamt.de/publikationen/entwicklung-eines-integrated-assessment-modells)

Poundstone, William: "Prisoners Dilemma"; 1992

Postman, Neil: "Amusing Ourselves to Death: Public Discourse in the Age of Show Business"; 2005

Sailer, Ulrich: "Management – Komplexität verstehen: Systemisches Denken, Business Modeling, Handlungsfelder nachhaltigen Erfolgs."; 2012

Senge, Peter M.: "The Fifth Discipline"; 2006

Senge, Peter et al: "The Necessary Revolution", 2010

Sheldrake, Rupert: "A new science of life - the hypothesis of morphic resonance;" 1981

Simon, Fritz B.: "Einführung in Systemtheorie und Konstruktivismus;" 2000

Sprockhoff, Harald von: "Bewußtsein, Geist und Seele;" 1996

Sterman, John D.: "Business Dynamics: Systems Thinking and Modeling for a Complex World"; 2000

Takeuchi, Nanoka: "The knowledge-creating company"; 1995

Taleb, Nassim Nicholas: "The Black Swan"; 2007

Trainer, Ted: "Can Renewable Energy Sustain a Consumer Society"

Vester, Frederic: "The Art of interconnected thinking: Tools and concepts for a new approach to tackling complexity"; 2007

Weggel, Oskar: "Die Asiaten"; 1989

Wilber, Ken: "A theory of everything"; 2001

Williams, Terry: "Modelling Complex Projects"; 2002

Wittgenstein, Ludwig: "Tractatus logico-philosophicus, Tagebücher und Philosphische Untersuchungen"; 1918

Wolpert, Lewis: "Six impossible things before breakfast"; 2007

Yourdon, Edward: "Death March"; 2003